Black Capitalism:
Problems in Development

Frederick E. Case

UCLA Housing, Real Estate and Urban Land Studies Program Series

The Praeger Special Studies program—utilizing the most modern and efficient book production techniques and a selective worldwide distribution network—makes available to the academic, government, and business communities significant, timely research in U.S. and international economic, social, and political development.

Black Capitalism:
Problems in Development

A Case Study of Los Angeles

PRAEGER SPECIAL STUDIES IN U.S. ECONOMIC AND SOCIAL DEVELOPMENT

Praeger Publishers   New York   Washington   London

PRAEGER PUBLISHERS
111 Fourth Avenue, New York, N.Y. 10003, U.S.A.
5, Cromwell Place, London S.W.7, England

Published in the United States of America in 1972
by Praeger Publishers, Inc.

Library of Congress Catalog Card Number: 72-82777

Printed in the United States of America

Black Capitalism was prepared under a grant from
The John Randolph Haynes and Dora Haynes Foundation,
Los Angeles, California.

HOUSING, REAL ESTATE AND URBAN LAND STUDIES PROGRAM
GRADUATE SCHOOL OF MANAGEMENT
UNIVERSITY OF CALIFORNIA, LOS ANGELES

The Housing, Real Estate and Urban Land Studies Program concerns itself with identifying and finding solutions to a wide range of problems related to urbanization by using a multidisciplinary approach to research that bears on the needs of the private as well as the public sector.

The program's staff includes UCLA faculty and graduate students who work as research assistants adding strength to their academic background.

The graduate course offerings emphasize the role of government and the public sector through housing courses, the role of business through a series of real estate and urban land economics courses; they stress the importance of solid theoretical underpinnings in both the public and private sectors in solving urban problems.

The program cooperates closely with the departments of economics, finance, political science, and geography and with the School of Engineering and the School of Architecture and Planning in research and course offerings.

The riots in South Central Los Angeles in 1965 focused national attention on the economic plight of black communities and subsequently fostered a rash of economic improvement programs. All kinds of public agencies and private organizations converged on Los Angeles with plans for improving the economic conditions of the central city inhabitants. In 1970 we suggested to the spokesmen for some of these agencies and organizations that an evaluation of their programs' effectiveness was long overdue, and they agreed. The Haynes Foundation trustees also agreed and provided funds for an in-depth analysis of efforts to revive the economic potential of the black community of South Central Los Angeles. Analysis was concentrated on two major goals—one to improve employment opportunities, the other to foster more black-owned and -operated businesses.

Initially, Los Angeles civic leaders were canvassed to determine which persons and organizations were most active in the central city economic revival program. Once we felt that we had a good representation of organizations and programs, we interviewed persons connected with them in-depth about what they were doing. We then turned to the black community to find out what had happened. This report reflects what program leaders said was being done and what black residents said had actually taken place over a period of more than five years of effort to increase the employment of the black population and the number of "black capitalists." The denouement is contained in this report.

Particular credit must be given to two persons who truly supplied the backbone of our research. Bob Edelen, a former corporate executive and local government official, took time off to concentrate on interviewing black businessmen and others who were to be the beneficiaries of the economic revival program. Through lengthy personal interviews and repeated visits he developed a series of revealing case studies on which our conclusions are based. He cannot be given enough credit for his outstanding contribution. George Anderson, a Ph.D. candidate in the Graduate School of Management, UCLA, was equally diligent in contacting civic leaders, the heads of programs intended to aid the black community, and others who could offer insights into how successfully South Central Los Angeles was recovering from the disastrous effects of the 1965 riots.

We have preserved the anonymity of the many black persons who contributed their histories and remained so patient during lengthy interviews. They spoke candidly and were most forceful in insisting that we report their views faithfully. We have tried to do so, hoping to convey the disillusionment and frustrations which so many feel. At the same time, we have tried to give an accurate account of what has and has not been done to assist the black community.

Compiling and editing the material has been difficult and time-consuming. Clearly there was an important message to be delivered on the problems involved in reviving the economic strength of an historically neglected black community. Both failures and successes had to be checked and rechecked to be sure that we had all the data and were interpreting them accurately. When the rough manuscript was finished, an outstanding effort was made by Harry Bain to organize and edit it so that it flowed well and developed its conclusions properly. He also added some background material from his own files.

Finally, someone had to decide what should or should not be included, and for this I accept full responsibility. It was not an easy task, but with the unstinting assistance of our program staff—Mrs. Rose Altman and Mrs. Alice Erickson—I was able to complete it. All of us hope that the high costs incurred in the course of the experiences that we report have not been in vain, and that our readers will profit as they join with us in seeking the economic revival of our urban minority communities.

CONTENTS

APPENDIXES

LIST OF TABLES

Black Capitalism:
Problems in Development

It began with an apparently routine traffic arrest on a hot August evening in 1965. Small crowds gathered and then began to swell alarmingly as rumors of police shootings of blacks fanned like brush fire through predominantly black South Central Los Angeles. With dismaying suddenness, these metaphorical fires became the real thing as crowds of angry blacks began putting the torch to buildings scattered throughout a 46-square-mile inner-city area that was soon to come under police and national guard curfew. The Watts riots had begun.

They lasted six days, claimed 34 lives, and produced 3,952 adult and juvenile arrests. Some 200 buildings went up in smoke at an estimated economic loss of $40 million. The psychological toll cannot be calculated, particularly since most Angelenos, black, white, or brown, had regarded their community as immune to this kind of violent disturbance. Their sense of security had rested on a shocking ignorance of the facts of life in Watts and its immediate environs.

Close observers had warned for some time of the explosiveness of a situation in which nearly 70 percent of Los Angeles County's 650,000 blacks were packed into the riot area. They had also called for programs to ease unemployment there, citing a jobless rate that was two to three times that of the surrounding white community. At the time of the upheaval, possibly 50,000 inner-city blacks and Mexican-Americans were out of work, and this despite an acknowledged shortage of skilled and semiskilled workers.

Aggravating the employment situation for residents of South Central Los Angeles was a woefully inadequate public transportation system. Employers were (and still are) scattered across the County's 450 square miles, and an average home-and-job round trip of 60 miles wasn't (and still isn't) unusual. With mass transit nonexistent, Southern Californians relied heavily on the automobile, an alternative especially disadvantageous to the inner-city poor.

3

Although insiders were well aware of the crisis in overcrowding, unemployment, and poor transportation in South Central Los Angeles, ordinary citizens may well have been lulled into a false sense of security by a 1964 Urban League survey of conditions for blacks in 68 American cities. Los Angeles was rated best in terms of housing, education, job opportunity, and other key indicators. At the same time that this survey was being reported, the future curfew area accounted for fully one-fourth of the County's annual $400 million welfare costs.

If the riots achieved nothing else, they touched off some of the most intense soul-searching in Los Angeles history. Why? What caused it? Who was responsible? What were the remedies? In the following months of accusations and laments, charges and countercharges, no one escaped unscathed. Agencies responsible for providing public services were alternately condemned and defended—the police, welfare, the schools—and, depending on the speaker of the moment, the residents of the riot area emerged as either wantonly violent and destructive or cruelly deprived and thus vindicated.

The millions of words of testimony and recommendations spawned what, in the beginning at least, seemed to be nearly as many private and public projects—invariably well-publicized—to improve the lot of the inner-city population. None was more highly touted or seemed more likely of general acceptance in the minority community than black capitalism. It was thought that the creation of black-owned and- operated businesses would at once provide jobs, foster pride, establish a stable black middle class, reduce the costs of public services, engender a desirable economic independence, and increase the level of income within the black community.

This study examines to what extent these early hopes have been borne out by experience with black capitalism projects in Los Angeles. Through case studies of black-owned enterprises and interviews with black businessmen, we have set out to measure not only how well the concept has lived up to its original promise, but also the performance of those agencies involved in stimulating the emergence of black capitalism.

THE ENVIRONMENT—1960 TO 1969

Before moving on to the major findings, it will be useful first to take a statistical look at employment trends in South Central Los Angeles in the five-year periods preceding and following the riots. What was the background of the disturbances? And what impact, if any, have post-disturbance projects had on the employment picture?

Changes—1960 to 1965

Between 1960 and 1965 in Los Angeles, the number of persons 14 years old and over declined about 8 percent, with the sharpest drop, 14 percent, occurring for men in South Central Los Angeles. The unemployment rate, reflecting national trends, declined from 10 to 8 percent. At the same time, labor force participation fell from 54 to 48 percent, and both men and women exhibited lower rates. This drop in participation was at odds with national trends and posed a difficult question for manpower experts.

Male labor force participation rates fell off most dramatically in the Watts section. Among males 14 years of age and over, the proportion seeking employment decreased from 78 to 58 percent. Only part of this decline could be attributed to relocations out of the area. The Bureau of Labor Statistics surmised that the situation was traceable to changing age distributions and an upsurge in school enrollments among young men.

Other contributing factors were that fewer men had families to support; some had not returned to the labor force since the 1965 riots eliminated their jobs, and the more successful jobseekers moved out of the area leaving behind a disproportionate number of those in ill health or otherwise unemployable. (Table 1 summarizes employment status in South Central and East Los Angeles between 1960 and 1965.)

Post-Riot Strategies

Faced with the manifest seriousness of the situation, local business leaders, along with state and federal agencies, launched a vigorous campaign to attack the root causes of the disturbances and revitalize the economic lives of South Central and East Los Angeles. In the main their efforts were concentrated on providing more and better jobs and increased opportunities for minority businessmen to enter managerial and entrepreneurial ranks.

(The numerous social, cultural, and general educational projects that went forward at the time are beyond the scope of this report. Their exclusion in no way minimizes their importance nor implies disagreement with the concept that urban problems should be attacked simultaneously on all levels—social, cultural, and economic.)

As in other cities that were wrestling with similar problems, economic programs in Los Angeles were both extensive and varied in their approaches. A few examples may serve to indicate what took place on a much wider scale.

One large bank initiated a policy to increase minority employment and simultaneously upgrade promotional opportunities for minority personnel. In 1968 alone this institution registered an 11 percent gain in minority placements while overall hiring increased only 2 percent. By 1968, blacks constituted 5 percent of the work force, all other minority groups 14 percent. Most importantly, the bank's strategy created openings and on-the-job training for persons formerly regarded as unemployable.

The Life Insurance Association of America and the American Life Convention responded to the crisis of the cities by embarking on a $1 billion venture to create housing and job opportunities in 227 cities. The sponsors reasoned that funds thus invested in job-creating programs would produce a multiplier effect far beyond the original investment. California received more benefits under the LIAA-ALC program than any of the other 41 states assisted.

TABLE 1

Employment Status of Persons in the Los Angeles UES Area, 1960 and November 1965

Employment status	Census of the Population 1960 (Persons 14 years of age and over)			Special Census Bureau Survey November 1965 (Persons 14 years of age and over)		
	Total	East Los Angeles	South Central	Total	East Los Angeles	South Central
BOTH SEXES						
Civilian noninstitutional population	83,207	45,253	37,954	76,660	42,880	33,780
Civilian labor force	44,937	24,980	19,957	36,550	21,330	15,220
Civilian labor force participation rate	54.0	55.2	52.6	47.7	49.7	45.1
Unemployed	4,598	2,071	2,527	3,050	1,500	1,550
Unemployment rate	10.2	8.3	12.7	8.3	7.0	10.2

6

MALE

Civilian noninstitutional population	38,874	21,482	17,392	34,830	19,800	15,030
Civilian labor force	29,340	16,420	12,920	23,260	13,820	9,440
Civilian labor force participation rate	75.5	76.4	74.3	66.8	69.8	62.8
Unemployed	3,064	1,431	1,633	1,960	980	980
Unemployment rate	10.4	8.7	12.6	8.4	7.1	10.4

FEMALE

Civilian noninstitutional population	44,333	23,771	20,562	41,830	23,080	18,750
Civilian labor force	15,597	8,560	7,037	13,290	7,510	5,780
Civilian labor force participation rate	35.2	36.0	34.2	31.8	32.5	30.8
Unemployed	1,534	640	894	1,690	520	570
Unemployment rate	9.8	7.5	12.7	8.2	6.9	9.9

Source: Urban Employment Studies, Regional Report 16, U.S. Dept. of Labor, Pacific Regional Office, San Francisco, California, July 1970.

7

Meanwhile the nation's savings and loan associations were enlarging their operations to provide new financial channels in core inner-city areas. At this writing, the Federal Home Loan Bank is processing applications for three inner-city savings and loans associations: two in Watts, one in East Los Angeles.

Nationwide, a number of private organizations have sprung up to meliorate the plight of the inner city. They include the National Alliance of Businessmen, the Urban Coalition, the Urban League, Urban America, and the Interracial Council of Business Organizations. The latter, known as ICBO, has been among the most significant organizations in Los Angeles. Others include the Management Council for Merit Employment, Training and Research (MC), the Small Business Administration (SBA), the Watts Labor Community Action Committee (WLCAC), the Los Angeles Urban Coalition (LAUC), and the Economic Resources Corporation (ERC).

In general, these organizations concentrate in Los Angeles upon management consulting, business counseling, and financial assistance to help ghetto businesses get started and achieve success. In many cases they call upon successful businessmen to volunteer their services in helping the minority entrepreneur set up or improve his business operations.

A basic goal is the encouragement of entrepreneurship within the inner city, and organizational efforts are frequently coordinated through SBA's Project Own, an activity whose objective was the creation of 20,000 minority-owned and operated businesses annually from fiscal year 1969 to the end of fiscal year 1970. SBA pursued this aim by forming minority entrepreneurship teams trained to offer assistance in the application for loans, the circumvention of bureaucratic obstacles, and the mastering of basic accounting and other procedures to assure receipt of loans.

In 1969 SBA made or guaranteed more than 4,300 minority loans valued at $101 million. But loss rates have run high, and the agency has tended to avoid financing high-risk small operations, which are typical of the inner-city commercial marketplace. Despite such disappointments, both public and private agencies are reaffirming their intention to institutionalize their programs so that training can be offered on an open and regular basis to anyone in the inner city (particularly anyone under 40) interested in starting a business or setting out toward an executive post in an existing business.

Post-Riot Employment Profile

After the riots, the hearings, the post-mortems by the experts, the anguished apologies by the newspapers, what happened? First of all, there was a great deal of well-intentioned finger pointing between the black and white communities, and within the majority community itself. Then there was equally well-intentioned planning, organization, and determination to remedy the ills that had led to the Watts catastrophe. The public image—and there was an abundance of publicity—was one of business and government rolling up their sleeves and combining to slay the dragons of discrimination, inadequate education, poverty, and privation.

By 1969, although unemployment rates for metropolitan Los Angeles and Long Beach had declined since 1965, the rate was up in South Central Los Angeles. The rate for black males was estimated at nearly 15 percent, for black females, about 18 percent. Clearly the job situation in the area *worsened* between 1965 and 1969. Thus in spite of a number of heroic efforts, the result was a continuing deterioration that yielded unemployment rates much higher than regional or national averages (Table 2).

If there was a silver lining, it lay in the assumption that many families had bettered their economic state and moved away from South Central Los Angeles. There was some support for this in the fact that 1969 found 38 percent more adult women than men in the 20-to-24-year-old group, suggesting an exodus of young males with better jobs. Even this explanation, however, cannot obscure the reality of pervasive poverty in South Central Los Angeles, where joblessness, at least in 1969, was almost triple the national level.

Improvement?

A 1970 Bureau of Labor Statistics report on employment and unemployment in East South Central Los Angeles, despite a certain lack of conformity with data compiled in 1960, 1965, and 1969, shows clearly that the 10 percent minority unemployment rate of 1960 still prevailed in 1969. It is even more discouraging to note that black employment fell from 90 percent in 1960 and 1965 to just under 84 percent in the last year of the decade.

We may well ask how this was possible with so many programs designed, and resources brought to bear, to improve conditions in the area. The present study sheds some light on a single aspect of the problem—the experience in promoting black capitalism. While some notable successes have been achieved, there is compelling evidence in our study that we still "have promises to keep and miles to go before [we] sleep."

One of our researchers, dismayed by the scant progress, asked if it were really in this case better "to light a candle than to curse the darkness." He wondered if the feeble light cast by our research wouldn't make the darkness of the problem even more terrifying, impenetrable, ungovernable. His answer, and ours, is that however discouraging initial studies may be, they are our only means for exposing the problem in all its dimensions and pointing the way toward a cure for the ills that stalk our decaying central cities.

There is no time to lose. As early as 1951, a committee of concerned Los Angeles citizens called attention to the urgent need for action to ease pressures in South Central Los Angeles. Their program had a substantially lower price tag than what has been spent in the area since 1965 or what was lost as a direct result of the riots—not to mention the loss of 34 lives and the incalculable toll in human misery from unrelenting poverty and privation.

Nor does the future promise a respite. In its *Research Report No. 3*, the Douglas Commission warns:

By 1985 the West will have replaced the Northeast as the most metropolitanized area in the country with 82 percent of its

TABLE 2

**Selected Characteristics of Jobseekers,
Civilian Labor Force, and Unemployed Persons, Los Angeles UES Areas,
July 1968-June 1969**

Characteristics	Jobseekers During Previous 12-Month Period	Civilian Labor Force		
		Total	Employed	Unemployed
TOTAL NUMBER[a]	13,000	37,700	33,800	3,900
Percent	100.0	100.0	100.0	100.0
Male	52.3	57.8	58.6	51.3
Female	47.7	42.2	41.4	48.7
16-19 years	30.0	11.7	8.9	35.9
20-44 years	53.8	56.5	57.4	48.7
45 years and over	16.2	31.8	33.7	15.4
In labor force at time of survey	80.0	100.0	100.0	100.0
Employed	51.5	89.7	100.0	—
Unemployed	28.5	10.3	—	100.0
Mexican-Americans[b]	34.6	47.7	50.0	28.2
Blacks	58.5	40.8	38.2	64.1

Household heads 20-64 years				
Male	40.0	53.3	56.2	30.8
Female	26.2	41.9	44.7	17.9
	13.8	11.4	11.5	12.8
With less than 4 years of high school	62.6	61.3	60.4	64.1
Occupation of present or last job				
White Collar	22.3	25.5	26.1	18.4
Blue Collar	49.2	56.2	57.6	47.4
Service	18.5	16.2	16.3	15.8
No previous work experience	10.0	1.9	—	18.4

a Besides Mexican-Americans and blacks, the total also includes a number of other whites, Japanese, Chinese, American Indians, and persons of other races not shown separately.
b Data are for all Spanish-Americans, most of whom are Mexican-Americans.

Source: See Table 1 in *Urban Employment Studies: Employment and Unemployment in East and South Central Los Angeles*, Regional Report No. 18, March 1971, p. 16.

inhabitants concentrated in SMSAs [Standard Metropolitan Statistical Areas]. Nonwhites who were more heavily concentrated in metropolitan areas than white in 1960 will be relatively even more concentrated by 1985. In 1985 almost four-fifths of all nonwhites in the United States will reside in SMSAs as contrasted with the seven-tenths of whites. In the West 90 percent or more of the nonwhite population will be found in SMSAs. The concentration of nonwhites in central cities within SMSAs will rise to a level of almost 58 percent from a level of 50 percent in 1960. In contrast, the concentration of white populations in central cities will diminish by almost a third to reach a level of 21 percent in 1985 from a level of 30 percent in 1960. Three-fifths or 59 percent of the nonwhites in the western states will be Central City residents. The trend projected here indicates that although there will be some decentralization of nonwhite population within the SMSAs, three-fourths or 75 percent of all nonwhites in metropolitan areas will still be residing in the Central City and only a fourth, or 25 percent, in the suburbs.

While all this remains a probability rather than a certainty, it would be unfortunate indeed if we were to ignore its implications. For in the meantime, there is every reason to believe that the lessons of Watts have produced little permanent positive change. In August 1970, the *Los Angeles Times* published this painful assessment:

> For the most part conditions blamed for the riots still exist and in some cases are worse (unemployment is now 16 percent compared to 10 percent in '65).

> Blacks living in what was the riot curfew area are divided on the questions of whether housing, education, health and welfare have improved since the riots.

> There are a few things on which almost all those recently interviewed by the Times did agree: crime is worse, narcotics flow is much freer, business is bad and those who can afford it are moving out.

A BASIS FOR EXAMINATION

Such reports can only be disillusioning to anyone who seeks improvement in the inner city. They are especially discouraging to those who have felt that black capitalism and increased employment opportunities for blacks would be sufficient to revive the flagging economic life of South Central Los Angeles.

This report, based on 11 case studies of black enterprises and interviews with knowledgeable black businessmen and administrators, will do little to alleviate such discouragement. The material gathered sheds light on what has succeeded and what hasn't, how black entrepreneurs define their problems, and how well they think public and private agencies are performing in nurturing the growth of black capitalism. In general, they are disappointed.

Our study findings are not necessarily representative of the situation in any or every inner city, nor can they be entirely accurate for South Central Los Angeles. Based as they are on interviews, the findings must necessarily reflect a strong subjective element. Nevertheless, there is convincing correlation with the findings of other studies: identical problems, strongly similar program approaches, the same difficulties in achieving solutions. Because of this common thread, we are convinced that some of the conclusions set forth in this report are true for the whole country. Others are peculiar to the Los Angeles milieu, and still others are so unusual that they defy even local classification. These last should receive further study, because they offer promising new directions toward correcting the shortcomings of existing programs for fostering black capitalism.

Two aspects of the study deserve special mention at this point. First, it is quite likely that in concentrating on the inner city, our research was dealing primarily with a problem of race. Findings bear out this hypothesis, and other research, principally by the Bureau of Labor Statistics, underscores the point by indicating that more and more blacks are moving to our inner cities. Thus the economic problems of these areas cannot be separated from the problems of race and poverty.

Secondly, it should be noted that we limited our investigation to programs of the SBA, ICBO, ERC, MC and the East Los Angeles Community Organization (ELACO). Preliminary studies had shown that the programs of these organizations were very representative of what was being done generally.

2

More often than not, discovering the need for black capitalism is an exercise in perspective. Much depends on one's angle of vision. For young Errold D. Collymore, Jr., a black Michigan State University graduate in business administration in 1961, black capitalism was the only escape from what he conceived as a "dehumanizing" future on a corporate treadmill made even less attractive by "pure and simple racism."

"There was no alternative," he writes in the April-May 1970 issue of the *MBA*. "I recognized that [having] my own business was the only vehicle under which responsible, paramount decisions could be made by me. I never made a recognizable decision worth anything while a corporation representative." [1] Now head of his own restaurant chain, Collymore spent seven years in the corporate ranks, mostly in personnel.

Thomas H. Kieren views "development of a managerial class and greater entrepreneurial effort" as no less important than education in "lifting the economic levels of minority people." Young, white, and a 1968 product of the University of Chicago Graduate School of Business, Kieren has been a volunteer consultant with the Talent Assistance Program (TAP) since 1969. Based in Chicago, TAP provides consulting services to both active and potential minority businessmen. Says Kieren, "What is needed for the development of a managerial and/or entrepreneurial class is an agent . . . for the dissemination of management education and guidance among talented minority group leaders." [2]

Black capitalism has its symbolic side, too. In *Negro Politics: The Search for Leadership*, James Q. Wilson reports on how one prominent Chicago black businessman viewed his success: "I think it's important to have demonstrations of the fact that Negroes have the ability to succeed, and that this demonstration of success is a form of race relations." [3] Militant criticism notwithstanding, the minority entrepreneur remains a potent opinion-molding force in his community.

Among today's minority college graduates, there is growing interest in entrepreneurship as a career. And emerging racial pride is only part of the reason; what Collymore calls "doing my own thing now" may be even more responsible for the popularity of the concept. In this regard, black capitalism is virtually identical to "calling my own shots," "being my own man," "go West, young man," or any of the other popular maxims that have historically characterized the individual's drive for independence.

If anything, today's entrepreneurial channels are even more treacherous to navigate than those of the past. Sterling H. Schoen and Wallace L. Jones sound this note of caution: "We look forward to seeing some of our black students ultimately strike out on their own to manage their own enterprises. This will not be easy. Not many white students do it, and we suspect that not many blacks will do it either. It is important, though . . . that those who wish to take the risk . . . be able to do so."[4]

Even such national authorities as Andrew F. Brimmer and Henry S. Terrell are dubious about the potential of black capitalism in the inner city. They expressed their skepticism in a paper presented in December 1969 before the annual meeting of the American Economic Association.[5] A year earlier, at the annual meeting of the American Real Estate and Urban Economics Association, Dr. Brimmer had issued a lukewarm assessment of the economic outlook for all-black banks.[6]

Caution and uncertainty are indeed alien to the aspirations of the six Los Angeles agencies treated in this report. Publicly and privately, they express decidedly more sanguine attitudes. Determination? Unquestionably. Racial pride? In almost every case. Hope for a better, more independent future? Unanimously. Social commitment? To a man. Preparation? Wholeheartedly. Interracial cooperation? Of course. Which brings us to the individual agencies.

THE ECONOMIC RESOURCES CORPORATION

This organization, known familiarly as ERC, was formed by Los Angeles business leaders with the support of the U.S. Department of Labor, the Office of Economic Opportunity, and the Economic Development Administration. ERC programs center about two major goals: creation of business opportunities for residents of the city's disadvantaged area, and the development of maximum new employment possibilities.

Watts Industrial Park, a 40-acre site, stands in the forefront of ERC's job creation program. To qualify for space in the development, industrial prospects must conform to current Fair Employment Practices hiring legislation and promote employment on all levels for residents of the immediate community. Moreover, tenancy must represent expansion and *new* employment causing no local employee displacement. There must also be training in skills to enhance worker mobility, opportunities for advancement, and no more than one employee for every 317 square feet of facility space.

ERC credits Watts Industrial Park with achieving the following substantial economic benefits, not only for residents of the disadvantaged area but for the community in general:

1. Creation of 2,670 jobs within the Park.

2. Creation of 4,025 jobs elsewhere in the target area.
3. Creation of a $43-million annual payroll.
4. Incrementation of local, state, and federal tax revenues by $10 million.
5. Incrementation of corporate and personal income tax revenues by $8 million.
6. Increase from $260,000 to $4 million in assessed value of land.
7. Increase from $30,000 to $480,000 in tax yield on land.
8. Reduction by $1,275,000 in welfare and unemployment expenses in the target community.

For minority entrepreneurs, ERC provides a battery of services extending from preferential business opportunities to marketing strategies for the sale of goods and services outside the impact area. Established or prospective entrepreneurs can obtain technical and management assistance, human relations counseling, advice on evaluating and executing floor leases, and working capital to meet short-term operating requirements.

INTERRACIAL COUNCIL FOR BUSINESS OPPORTUNITY

Formed originally in 1963 in New York City, this organization has since become national with local ICBO councils in Los Angeles, New Orleans, Newark, St. Louis, and Washington, D.C. Numerous other cities are joining the ranks at this writing. To facilitate its goal of creating, expanding, and improving minority-owned businesses, ICBO relies on a three-pronged approach: helping to make credit available to black enterprises; maintaining a full-range consulting program to assist clients in establishing and managing their own businesses; and setting up educational programs to improve minority enterprises.

ICBO has aided more than 2,000 small businesses and helped to generate some $5 million in small business loans in minority areas across the country. Through the $3-million ICBO Fund, Inc., the organization acts in concert with four major New York City banks to furnish partial guarantees for "soft" loans to minority entrepreneurs. In all cases where financing is the objective, ICBO works through local council banking and credit committees to assist clients.

The New Enterprise Program, launched in 1968 to foster and develop businesses with a minimum capitalization of $100,000, operates in conjunction with Project Transfer to move inner-city enterprises from white to black hands. But New Enterprise also stresses the support of activities that can prosper beyond the confines of the ghetto. In its first six months, the program processed 75 proposals, including a $100,000 computer systems corporation, a $400,000 cosmetic supply house, and a $6-million motel.

Management Courses

Recently, a Los Angeles ICBO official commented, "Helping someone succeed in business frequently calls for much more than locating a site, obtaining financing, getting credit with suppliers or building up a clientele. The critical missing ingredient is often the client's lack of practical basic information about what it takes to run a business smoothly and profitably."

To deal with this problem, ICBO and its councils have developed courses in the fundamentals of business practice. Typically, the program involves cooperative arrangements between ICBO councils and colleges and universities in their respective cities. Management seminars are offered in such subjects as accounting, business law, credit, sales promotion and marketing, production, advertising, and personnel management. At this writing, more than 1,500 men and women from all over the country have attended ICBO courses.

Volunteer Consultants

The heart of the ICBO program is volunteer consulting services. The consultants, both black and white, span the full spectrum of business expertise, work with clients on a one-to-one basis, and serve without pay. There are more than 200 in Los Angeles alone, drawn from banks, campuses, aerospace firms, accounting firms, and a host of other commercial enterprises.

Clients may be seasoned businessmen or anxious newcomers. After their applications for assistance are evaluated, each is assigned to a consultant whose business background and experience corresponds to his own needs. Typically, the association is a durable one, often lasting a year or more. In effect, the consultant becomes a business counselor who can call in other consultants whenever the need arises. Los Angeles case histories reveal that as many as five consultants may work with the same client at the same time.

Their services, like all those offered by ICBO, are free to the client. The aim is to foster minority business in the belief that this will create for the minority community enormous economic and social benefits. Of the latter, our Los Angeles ICBO executive said, "The relative absence of successful Negro businessmen has a negative influence on the Negro American community and the nation . . . It deprives the community of an essential symbol of full participation in American life and means that a large segment of our population is denied understanding of the free enterprise system."

ICBO in Los Angeles

A Black-Owned Department Store

This enterprise, specializing in the sale of women's apparel, was purchased with an SBA-guaranteed loan of $27,000. ICBO helped the owner in arranging the factoring of his accounts receivable and in establishing a line of credit with a local bank. A recent audit disclosed that the business is maintaining a five-figure cash flow, operating ratios are being held, and sales are measuring up to initial projections.

An Industrial Services Firm

ICBO helped obtain the financing that launched this company in 1969. It has contracts for telephone booth maintenance and repair in South Central Los Angeles and for the refurbishing of telephone parts and cords. ICBO assisted in negotiating agreements with Pacific Telephone and Telegraph and Western Electric, and at the time of this survey was counseling on additional service contracts. The firm operates a fleet of four specially equipped trucks for cleaning and employs 14 full-time and 4 part-time former "hard-core unemployables."

Backing the Fruits of Invention

One of ICBO's first clients was a black inventor who had perfected a highly competitive, portable, stereo record player. Working with volunteer consultants, he devised a strategy that would enable him to finance production of his invention while retaining effective control of the enterprise. ICBO assisted him in applying for an SBA loan and raising an additional $100,000 from private sources. Production has begun, and the owner was expecting to provide at least 200 jobs for unskilled minority workers by 1970.

A Wood Products Venture

This company, capitalizing initially by an ICBO-guaranteed loan of $25,000, began operations with the manufacture of baseball bats. When market projections proved overly optimistic, the firm diversified by developing a line of sandboxes, picnic tables, pool tables, toy chests, and easels for sale through established retail outlets. Additional funding of $450,000 was obtained through an SBA-guaranteed loan in 1968. The firm was employing 23 "unemployables" at the time of the survey.

THE LOS ANGELES URBAN COALITION

This group styles itself "a unique type of organization" that is "trying to collect the best Los Angeles leadership talent and put it to work to solve the urban crisis." Its approach seems to begin with high-level sessions in which government, business, and educational leaders gather to try and place their collective fingers on precisely what is ailing inner-city Los Angeles.

Having settled the question of causes and cures, they become "catalysts" who generate community concern and influence the appropriate institutions to undertake solutions. Thereupon LAUC exchanges its catalyst role for that of "coordinator," by which it "obtains necessary corrective action through private and public organizations."

If well-known Los Angeles names are any guarantee of success, LAUC— and the disadvantaged communities—have nothing to worry about. Among its faithful it numbers Mayor Sam Yorty, Councilman Thomas Bradley, Rabbi Paul Dubin, Father Charles S. Casassa, John McCone, Louis Lundborg, Daniel Bryant, and Frederick Schnell. McCone heads the Joshua Hendy Corporation, while Schnell is senior vice president of Prudential Insurance Company. Lundborg only recently stepped down as board chairman of Bank of America, and Bryant directs the affairs of the Bekins Company.

LAUC firmly supports the concept of rapidly expanding business opportunities in minority communities and is especially interested in a Nixon Administration plan to divert a portion of federal business to minority-owned companies. Not surprisingly, it is also solidly behind a local set-aside program for Los Angeles and is soliciting the cooperation of numerous public and private groups how best to plan and carry out such a venture.

THE MANAGEMENT COUNCIL FOR MERIT EMPLOYMENT TRAINING AND RESEARCH*

Organized in response to the Watts riots, MC concentrates almost exclusively on bringing together qualified workers from disadvantaged areas and employers with jobs to fill. Working through more than 1,200 firms and 15 affiliated employer groups, MC encourages employers to reach into ghetto neighborhoods to seek out, recruit, and hire minority candidates.

Experience has convinced MC that inadequate education or lack of job skills, or both, are often the most formidable barriers separating the unemployed from a weekly paycheck. To remove this shortcoming, MC makes every effort to arrange training for those who require it at one of the city's numerous skills centers or adult vocational schools. (Appendix B provides a brief discussion of the activities of one such skill center.)

Financing for these programs has come from a variety of sources, including the aerospace industry, the Ford Foundation, the Haynes Foundation, private industry, and other foundations and associations. Funds have been used to secure high-level program commitment from private industry and to cement relations with numerous minority organizations and individuals.

In addition to its role as moral persuader and educational coordinator, MC has undertaken periodic surveys to determine how much progress has been made in opening job opportunities to minority workers. The last, in November 1966, disclosed that 201 corporate respondents had placed 17,903 minority applicants since August 1965, the month of the riots.

THE WATTS LABOR COMMUNITY ACTION COMMITTEE

From a small beginning of five people and a treasury of $4, nonprofit WLCAC has grown since 1965 into a near-conglomerate with a staff of 120 and

---

*Taken from *Southern California Business*, Los Angeles Chamber of Commerce, XXXII, No. 15.

three subsidiaries: Greater Watts Development Corporation (nonprofit), Greater Watts Construction Co. (profit), and Greater Watts Enterprises, Inc. (profit).

The organization's original purpose in early 1965 was to beautify Watts and transform the community into the kind of neighborhood in which individuals of any life style would be happy to live. With the riots, an already firm commitment to the concept of minority economic power was strengthened still further. Timely federal funding, general community support, and interest-free loans from trade unions have made it possible for WLCAC to mount a vigorous and diversified black capitalism program.

The organization has invested in a service station, a restaurant, farm land, a poultry ranch, and four grocery markets. It is also planning a senior citizens' housing center and a child day care facility. Supplementing these activities are training programs of various kinds that serve some 1,700 local residents annually. Anyone meeting the poverty criterion qualifies to take part in such programs.

WLCAC makes no direct loans to entrepreneurs who wish to start or expand their own businesses. Its policy is that the community's best interests will be served if the group maintains a tight grip on assets and earnings, controls its own enterprises, and makes sure that business proceeds do not trickle away into other sections of the city.

THE SBA: ONCE OVER LIGHTLY

Created as an independent government agency by Congress in 1953, SBA works through its network of state and territorial field offices to provide for small businesses such services as lease guarantees, management assistance, various types of counsel loans, counseling, and aid in obtaining government contracts. The agency publishes and disseminates more than 800 documents covering successful practices in virtually every small business field.

Most small businesses, except for gambling or speculative firms, newspapers, and radio and TV stations, are eligible for SBA loans. In establishing such eligibility, the agency adheres to these general criteria:

1. Wholesale—annual sales from $5 million to $15 million, depending on the industry.

2. Retail or service—annual sales or receipts from $1 million to $5 million, depending on the industry.

3. Construction—annual sales or receipts of not more than $5 million averaged over a 3-year period.

4. Manufacturing—from 250 to 1,500 employees, depending on the industry.

SBA administrators may choose among several media in providing financial assistance to small businessmen. There are direct and immediate participation loans, pool loans, loans to state and local development companies, lease guaranty programs, and direct loans and guarantees to Small Business Investment Companies (SBICs) that in turn provide venture capital to eligible small firms.

For purposes of this report, two SBA programs are of direct concern, the Economic Opportunity Loans (EOL) and the Minority Enterprise Program. Both bear importantly upon the establishment and vital early support of minority-operated enterprise and, in this sense, take priority here over the less immediate benefits of Section 8A.

ECONOMIC OPPORTUNITY LOANS

These provide both management and financial assistance, the latter as much as $25,000 for up to 15 years. Both prospective and established small businessmen are eligible for assistance, provided (1) their family income from all sources other than welfare is insufficient for basic family needs; (2) through social or economic disadvantage they have been unable to acquire business financing through normal lending channels on reasonable terms. Applicants must also demonstrate satisfactory management ability and provide reasonable assurance that business earnings will be adequate to repay the loan.

MINORITY ENTERPRISE PROGRAM

Begun in 1968 in concert with banks, private industry, and local communities, this program marks the first time that all SBA services have been brought together in a coordinated thrust to close a gap that finds all ethnic minorities owning only 3.25 percent of the nation's more than 5 million small businesses.

"Recruiting" of those with a desire for ownership and with management aptitude is carried out principally through regional offices and "outreach" centers in areas of heavy minority concentration. SBA field representatives work closely with community action groups in identifying potential entrepreneurs and circulating information on ME programs.

Once a candidate is located, the field representative in effect becomes his business advocate by locating a sound opportunity, providing assistance on financial statements and business projections, preparing the loan application, etc. There is heavy emphasis on technical and management assistance, since survey findings have shown that faulty management is to blame in more than one of out of every ten new business failures.

SBA policy is to process ME loans under relaxed eligibility criteria that place the heaviest emphasis on the applicant's character and ability to repay from the profits of the business. While SBA is authorized to make direct loans, most transactions are through private banks with the agency guaranteeing up to 90 percent. The average such loan is about $20,000 with a term of from five to six years.

Experience to date has shown that most minority business opportunities, whether new or established, are in retailing, distributing, franchising, and service industries. SBA, however, does officially encourage diversification and works with local groups in forming development companies and SBICs to achieve that end. The agency is also quick to point out its increasing activity in coordinating efforts by minority entrepreneurs to take advantage of Section 8A.

IT'S IN THE HELPING

Even the brief overview in this chapter cannot obscure the fact that there should be considerable assistance available to the budding or budded entrepreneur in Los Angeles. Money. Counseling. Continuing education. Preferential position on public contracts. And more. All the hopeful aspirant, whatever his color, has to do is pick up his newspaper and read about what is being accomplished.

But is it? If Los Angeles is representative of what has been going on elsewhere in the country, then there is more a chasm than a gap between performance and publicity. In fact, the publicity emerges as a major source of irritation among applicants for the various programs. We turn in the remainder of this report to an examination of minority capitalism through the eyes of prominent authorities and practicing businessmen. We shall see that the proof of the help, now and always, is in the size of the helping.

NOTES

1. Errold D. Collymore, Jr., "Entrepreneurship: Alternative or Necessity," *MBA* (April-May 1970), p. 54.

2. Thomas H. Kieren, "Consulting for Minority Enterprise," *Issues/ Ideas*, XVIII, 1, (Summer 1970), 52-52.

3. James Q. Wilson, *Negro Politics: The Search for Leadership* (New York: The Free Press, 1960).

4. Sterling H. Schoen and Wallace L. Jones, "The Consortium: A Progress Report," *MBA* (April-May 1970), p. 47.

5. Andrew F. Brimmer and Henry S. Terrell, "The Economic Potential of Black Capitalism," paper given at 82nd meeting of the American Economic Association, New York, 1969.

6. Andrew F. Brimmer, "The Banking System and Urban Economic Development," *Proceedings of the American Real Estate and Urban Economics Association*, 1968.

3

ISOLATING
THE MAJOR
TROUBLE SPOTS

In Los Angeles, as in other major cities around the country, the grand strategy for the war on the economic problems of the disadvantaged has assigned prominent roles to job training and placement and to the creation of minority entrepreneurship opportunities. While evaluation of Los Angeles job programs was largely beyond the scope of this study, those minority entrepreneurs interviewed repeatedly stressed their recognition of the need for such programs.

On the national level, there is incomplete but growing evidence that both employment and entrepreneurship efforts are failing. These early returns question not only the performance of established programs, but also the efficacy of the minority capitalism concept itself. Listen to what Andrew F. Brimmer and Henry S. Terrell had to say in a recent study:

> In the long run, the pursuit of Black Capitalism may retard the Negroes' economic advancement by discouraging many from the full participation in the national economy with its much broader range of challenges and opportunities. In spite of this fact, Black Capitalism may also prove to be deleterious to the Negro community because, in the words of true observers, "The program would place those least capable of accepting risks in the position of accepting larger risks." New ghetto enterprises would certainly be more prone to failure than already-established firms and their failures would have a lasting burden on the individual starting these firms and on those employees that have been induced to work in such enterprises, rather than in businesses not dependent on the ghetto economy. A solution to the economic problems of Negroes and other disadvantaged groups is a complex and difficult task. Efforts must be made on a variety of fronts, and a choice of a mix of programs must be made quite carefully.[1]

The high failure potential of ghetto enterprise cited by Brimmer and Terrell was underscored in this gloomy assessment by the *Wall Street Journal*:

Today's self-employment opportunity for the black man all too
often turns out to be a dubious, slum-oriented franchise, light industry or retail outlet. It should not be surprising that many of these
enterprises have failed for reasons that include a surfeit of enthusiasm but not too much sound business or management experience.
Witness the recent failure of Julian Bond and Gerald Reed, a white
dentist, to create a Black-controlled restaurant chain. It appears,
although there may have been many other factors as well, that a
complete lack of managerial skill and prior comparable business
experience contributed heavily to the collapse.[2]

The "surfeit of enthusiasm," all too readily stoked by the invariable
outpouring of overreaching press releases, creates at least two major problems.
First, it diverts attention from the underlying and persistent obstacles that
must be identified and overcome if minority capitalism is to become a viable
economic remedy. Secondly, it causes profound disillusionment when economic realities fail to keep pace with early promises. This, in turn, leads to
mistrust in the community and an unwillingness among potential entrepreneurs
to take part in the programs.

An example of this Pollyanna outlook was "Black Capitalism on the
Move," an article written by Carl T. Rowan and David M. Macie for the
February 1969 *Reader's Digest*. The authors implied strongly that all that was
really required to make capitalism work was for inner-city blacks to get
together and collectively develop businesses and other activities. The theme of
the article was that self-help would overcome all obstacles.

After a year spent talking to struggling Los Angeles minority entrepreneurs and studying their operations, our researchers developed little toler-
ance for what they came to call "the *Reader's Digest* syndrome." Their
experience convinced them that such self-help efforts were simply not equal to
the task. Robert Edelen, a former public relations executive, put it this way:

How can a man who has been chronically unemployed and who lives
in an area where there are practically no markets even acquire the
understanding that there might be a possibility of his starting a
business? Or, if he already has a business, how can he possibly
succeed, given the narrow profit margin and the lack of consumers
available in his market area. In an age when people are aggressively
searching for business opportunities and cannot find them in South
Central and East Los Angeles, then these business opportunities
simply do not exist. Believe me, it's no coincidence that we discovered a limited array of retail services in South Central areas. There
just is no market for such services.

Publications of the Small Business Administration tend to support
Edelen's view and cast doubt on the *Reader's Digest* syndrome philosophy that
enthusiasm and self-help are sufficient. According to SBA literature, the following conditions are the ones that create the most serious problems for active or
prospective minority businessmen.

1. Lack of individual qualifications.
2. Lack of a business heritage.
3. Lack of opportunity.
4. Lack of capital.
5. Lack of business know-how.

Turning to the minority enterprise itself, the SBA cites these obstacles as commonplace:

1. The business is generally marginal.
2. It is undercapitalized.
3. It is limited to retail or service.
4. It is highly vulnerable to vandalism and pilferage.
5. The owner(s) cannot obtain business insurance.
6. Its locational opportunities are restricted.
7. It can appeal only to limited markets.
8. It must rely on unskilled personnel.

This survey uncovered nothing to discredit the SBA's view of the situation. Our findings argue persuasively that a major barrier to encouraging minority business and employment lies in a failure to appreciate the fact that the problem is one of *race* and of *location within a poor economic market*. The findings also suggest that government and private efforts are not really responsive to these conditions and those others identified by the SBA and the Brimmer-Terrell study.

A DISSENTING VIEWPOINT

Professor Richard N. Farmer concurs that the programs are not responsive, but he has his own theory about what corrective steps should be taken. Writing in Indiana University's *Business Horizons*, Farmer draws an analogy between foreign aid ventures and efforts to promote minority enterprise. "The wrong model has been applied to the problem," he insists, "and, as a result, all the wrong variables are dealt with."

Farmer believes that the real problem can be traced to an inability of small businessmen to use capital wisely. While they may be good technicians (that was what got them into the business), Farmer feels that they are poor managers who keep poor records, do little planning, and depend upon control systems that are inoperable.

His solution would be to begin with a modest program without the large funds that attract those who tend to spend not wisely but too well. In Farmer's program, the emphasis would be on practical business training for both existing and potential small business. This predilection seems to trace to his research in Indianapolis where he found a real demand for such programs and to his own view of what is essential to promote minority enterprise.

To accomplish his program, Farmer recommends the use of an available but overlooked pool of college-trained manpower—students in the schools of business. (In a later section, we shall see that such students may be of little real value in solving the problems of ghetto businessmen.) Even with training, however, Farmer is less than sanguine about the prospects of achieving a massive improvement in the minority ownership pattern in business. He suggests that the real problem is the difficulty in entering *any* business.

While there is a certain merit in Professor Farmer's recommendations, his views are clearly at odds with those of Dr. Brimmer, not simply regarding the scope of what must be done, but also in their respective interpretations of the root causes of the problem.

Brimmer's vision is on a more cosmic scale and leads him to argue that success in developing minority capitalism lies ultimately in ensuring that minority business share in total economic activity at a ratio roughly equal to the representation of minorities in the population.

Our own research tends to confirm Brimmer's assessment. In a large city like Los Angeles, the magnitude of the problem is already such that Farmer's tactics would probably impress minority entrepreneurs as a largely irrelevant, token gesture, given the depth and urgency of the situation. The minority entrepreneurs interviewed during this study were often outspokenly bitter over the gap between promise and performance in encouraging economic revival in the central city.

CENTRAL CITY BUSINESSMEN SOUND OFF—A CONSENSUS

Ask a minority businessman in Central Los Angeles what business assistance programs have been of greatest value to him, and he is almost certain to reply, "Very few or none at all." In our interviews, this response was all but unanimous, and it was typically rendered with undisguised resentment and hostility. Many businessmen insisted that even those firms that did receive aid would still have received it whether or not the agencies were in existence.

Our own case studies, even after repeated analysis, fail to divulge any reliable explanation of why some firms received help and others did not. There are no acceptable criteria to show why a box-maker or macaroni manufacturer, to cite two examples, received assistance while it was denied to a firm dealing in electronic devices. The data on lending to minority businesses were so scattered and incomplete that they defied rigorous definition of the criteria used to determine eligibility for assistance.

Perhaps the most important finding is that the agencies use risk evaluation criteria that are almost identical with those applied by conventional lending institutions. This means, of course, that the agencies are not taking the kind of risks or seeking the quality of risks that were anticipated at the outset of the programs. For their part, central city businessmen seem unrealistically blind to the policies and programs of the various agencies and their associated forms and other administrative procedures. When it comes to what lenders will lend and what borrowers hope to receive, the agencies and their clients are clearly traveling separate roads. This divergence of opinion is symptomatic of a disquieting lack of communication and understanding uncovered by the survey between agencies and their actual and potential clients. Its legacy is an even more disquieting resentment that prompted many respondents to brand all agency lending programs as "hoaxes," "farces perpetrated upon black people," or "big do-nothings." Warranted or not, these remarks indicate a smoldering frustration among central city entrepreneurs who see themselves standing by powerlessly as their community declines.

Although the case studies concentrate heavily on the black community, there is evidence that the same frustration, respecting no racial or ethnic boundaries, is as prevalent in Los Angeles' Mexican-American neighborhoods. An East Los Angeles mattress plant, set up through widespread community involvement and a $10,000 interest-free loan from a foundation, has enjoyed reasonable success but is floundering in its efforts to locate new sources of funding.

If this study fails to throw a spotlight on the exact process by which some firms and individuals were either favored or bypassed by assistance, it did reveal some clues that may serve as points of departure for additional research. For one thing, it seems clear that traditional minority businesses—consumer service and retail—are neither encouraged nor supported. For another, it appears equally clear that a firm must employ between 9 and 15 persons to receive consideration for eligibility. Yet whenever the researchers began to feel they had identified a common thread, they would encounter a firm that seemed to qualify in every respect and which nevertheless received no assistance. The unpredictability and lack of consistent policy in administering minority assistance programs made for a disconcerting research experience.

Equally disconcerting is our suspicion, strengthened almost daily over the course of our investigation, that many of those active in promoting minority enterprise have yet to face up to the fact that the small businessman, as such, is on the endangered species list. If this suspicion accurately reflects the realities, and we strongly believe it does, then any programs that play down the crucial role of education and experience in achieving business success do a real disservice to our minority citizens.

There is likewise too little straight talk on just what it takes to get established and how trying and risky the process may be. Too often the minority small businessman comes up with an idea and sets up an embryonic business in anticipation of getting financing from some public or private agency. This is usually denied him, for any one of a variety of reasons, and it is surely unfortunate that too little effort is made at this point to redirect him.

It is no less unfortunate that some early warning mechanism did not exist at the outset to evaluate and set forth what the agencies consider a reasonable business prospectus and acceptable level of operations. Such precautions are mandatory, for when the risks of financing small businesses are combined with the ethnic factor, the total risk may well intimidate even an agency committed to facing high-risk ventures.

BLACK EXECUTIVES VIEW THE LOS ANGELES SCENE

H. Chad McClellan would have felt at home under Secretary John Gardner of the Department of Health, Education and Welfare in the Kennedy Administration. The Secretary liked to surround himself with "dynamos," and McClellan might have put even that cliché to an acid test. He has been prominent in Los Angeles in most efforts to revive the central city, and his preference for mobilizing volunteer efforts is reflected in his service with the Interracial Council for Business Opportunities and the Management Council. He is particularly emphatic about the need for training, jobs, and expanded business opportunities.

Robert Edelen, quoted earlier in this chapter, did a great deal of listening during the year he spent interviewing people for this study. He found out that most efforts in Los Angeles were being directed toward creation of job opportunities and the development and support of minority enterprise. He also became increasingly pessimistic about the programs themselves and their re-sults. Between them, McClellan and Edelen pretty well sum up the problems of launching and sustaining minority enterprise in Los Angeles.

The Publicity Albatross

"The publicity on efforts to help the inner city is excessive," Edelen says flatly. Generally, he thinks that the agencies have produced far more press releases than results. "For example, the SBA, the Economic Resources Corpora-tion and the ICBO have become widely known for their efforts to promote minority capitalism and jobs. But the total of those efforts is far short of what is needed and in many ways seems far short of the resources expended."

Make no mistake—a great deal of publicity has been, and is being, released about what is taking place in South Central and East Los Angeles. To the agencies' credit, they are generally displeased by all this attention. Nevertheless, a general feeling has developed that much is being accomplished for the minority citizens of Los Angeles.

However, despite diligent and repeated efforts, our researchers were un-able to come up with the kind of reliable quantitative data required for any valid assessment of progress. They did unearth an imposing list of firms all of which absolutely refused to be interviewed, simply because they had endured intolerable frustration in their attempts to work with various assistance agencies.

These companies could see nothing to be gained by cooperating with our own or any other research effort, for they saw no reason why their histories should offset an already strongly entrenched public image. And the firms that did agree to take part did so only on the stipulation that their views and experiences would be reported accurately and in full. They made no bones about their intention to "tell it like it is," so that others might discover in advance what the real problems were.

(Perhaps the most arresting characteristic of the managers in this latter group is that they were powerfully motivated by an entrepreneurial instinct that drove them to "do their own thing." In this context, the reader will recall the statement by Errold Collymore, the young black restauranteur introduced in the opening paragraphs of Chapter 2. Our Los Angeles sample felt it was neither possible nor practicable for others generally to follow their example. For them individually, however, it was the accepted course of action.)

The Relentless Pursuit of Capital

Edelen says, "The assumption is without foundation that giving black businessmen good management or business practice advice will overcome their chronic lack of capital. They know they need capital but are unable to acquire it." Edelen disputes what he calls the "general agreement" among agencies and influential whites that minority owners are incapable of running their own businesses. He maintains that many of these owners have stayed afloat for years, despite small profits, and have avoided the failures predicted by some lenders and supporters of the minority capitalism concept.

For Edelen, the tight profit margins common to inner-city businesses are more a result of undercapitalization than of minority administration. The chief problem, he insists, is the resulting inability to purchase whatever goods and services are needed to achieve more profitable levels of production or sales. But when a minority entrepreneur approaches an assistance agency or lending institution, Edelen feels he is passing into a virtual never-never land.

"The experience of minority businessmen in seeking loans through SBA, ERC, Bank of America, United California Bank and other lenders has been most discouraging," Edelen reports. "After a year of negotiating, many are still awaiting approval of their first loans. They speak of spending endless hours at meetings where they are continually subjected to analysis and critiques, only to be turned down for seemingly trivial reasons. For this and other reasons, the people I talked to see the whole lending process as a constant harrassment in which there is little hope funds will be available when needed."

To put it as charitably as possible, this study offers a strong case that lending institutions have not sufficiently adapted themselves to be effective in fostering minority capitalism in the inner city. While it is true that the fiduciary relationship between banking officials and depositors requires the former to swallow hard when faced with high-risk, low-profit, inner-city ventures, this fact of financial life in no way lessens the need for capital in the central core. Reluctantly, our research compels us to conclude that high-risk loans, in the volume needed by minority entrepreneurs, are not available through the present banking structure.

What then of the agencies themselves? Edelen is no more cheerful on this point. His indictment is both general and specific. "Among black businessmen who have attempted to work with federal agencies, and among others who are trying to do something to improve the central city business climate, there is an attitude that a variety of agencies are using minority capitalism as a stalking horse to trap an unwarranted share of federal grants for projects that ultimately will not pay off."

Edelen further charges that these agencies, through well-paid administrators and staffs, project a persuasive aura of wanting to assist minority businessmen, but that their concrete accomplishments are very poor proof of their good intentions. Returning to the problem of publicity, he notes, "SBA loans, for example, are highly publicized, but many minority applicants see the amount of political pull necessary to obtain them as far beyond their scope."

On the surface at least, Edelen sees federal programs as a bright source of hope for the inner city. But his research has persuaded him that these funds, ever in short supply, are being devoted to causes that are both unrelated to central city economic needs and burdened with a much higher risk factor than opportunities available in the minority business community.

"There are many struggling minority enterprises unable to secure any form of federal assistance," he says. "And they pose less risk than many projects already being sponsored by federal dollars. These latter persist because, unfortunately, there are still enough would-be entrepreneurs who hope to get something out of the agencies by cooperating and helping give the appearance of success that is crucial to justifying the agencies' continued existence."

Edelen reports that minority businessmen dismissed the Economic Resources Corporation as a failure. "The minority businessman typically lacks assets to pledge as loan security," Edelen observes, "but when ERC makes a loan, it requires the borrower to pledge all his personal assets. If a personal crisis arises later, the borrower is stripped of any assets that might furnish collateral to tide him over.

"Minority entrepreneurs have decided that ERC will lend only to those whose assets are sufficient to cover losses from a business failure and whose enterprises promise high profit potential." Edelen's experience leads him to believe that although there are a number of blacks in decision-making posts within ERC, there is suspicion among minority businessmen about their ability to influence final judgments. "Individually, each of these men expresses strong belief in what ERC is doing," he says. "But this is apparently because of the benefits they see for themselves rather than the benefits they see going to the black community as the result of ERC activities."

(The major ERC activity has been creation of the Watts Industrial Park described in Chapter 2. While the agency claims imposing benefits in new jobs and business opportunities, Edelen says only, "Ironically, the park is situated within the bounds of the all-white city of Lynwood and is not readily accessible either to black entrepreneurs or the black population seeking employment.")

Chad McClellan knows all there is to know when it comes to locating financing for minority enterprise. In Los Angeles he has acquired a reputation as a doer. Not surprisingly, his views of the lending process in the inner city are not identical with those expressed by Robert Edelen. When asked, "There has been a lot of talk about negative attitudes of banking. Is this an accusation with merit?" he answered:

> That isn't the problem. You have to recognize the bankers' position. I wouldn't think of going to a bank to fund some of the deals we've been discussing. The banks have offered quite a little money if we need it. They have provided quite a few funds for operations, and they have helped in the community. But I wouldn't go to the bank, any bank, and say, "This is a loan that I would recommend your

bank make." The loan just doesn't meet their criteria for a legitimate loan. What we have to do is create a special high-risk, low-interest, long-term fund for the specific purpose we have in mind. I am not willing to help a business secure such funds unless I believe it has at least a 60 percent chance of success.

In general McClellan is far less critical of agency performance than Edelen. To McClellan, capital is but one "ingredient," albeit an important one, in the overall evaluation of minority business prospects for success. He furnished this brief case history in illustration of his point:

One man came to us a year ago and wanted to go into the manufacturing business. I was greatly impressed because he was intelligent and well educated, although he did not have management experience. I pointed this out to him and encouraged him to include someone with management experience, because it was obvious that he could promote but couldn't operate too well by himself.

The business venture he had in mind was pretty ambitious. He had already raised quite a little money but had not yet made an analysis of what he would manufacture. I asked him if he would accept a feasibility study because of the potential scale of his planned operations. He agreed and I helped him get a $10,000 study made that cost him nothing. It was an excellent document. I went over it myself with the researcher who made the study.

In the meantime, the man starting the business drew about him some others who were competent, had lots of initiative and were very persuasive. They went on their way regardless of the counsel that I gave or that was in the document I had provided. Unfortunately, the results were precisely what we had cautioned they would be unless they followed the procedures prescribed in the study.

They raised a lot of money, $150,000 from one source. At the end of the line they discovered that what was in the feasibility study in the first place was accurate, and they had to start all over. At this point they had spent the $150,000 they had obtained.

They had switched into a different kind of production and were operating with modest success, having sold a very substantial amount of products in advance of manufacturing with the idea that they would convert to that type of production. But now they were in the position where they had spent the money, had none in the bank, had tens of thousands of dollars in orders that they could not fill and had no money to produce the products that were sold by these orders.

This situation illustrates vividly what I am talking about when I say that the ingredients—the criteria under which the enterprise begins—

must include all of the fundamentals (1) feasibility in terms of market and manufacturing (2) the competence and the responsibility of those involved to deal appropriately with funds (3) a means to get the kind of counsel that corporations get from a board of directors or from tax counsel or from their attorney or whomever. Unless these ingredients are available, any enterprise has too small a chance to succeed. Even with all the factors, about 90 percent of the new businesses will fail.

McClellan's anecdote reveals his own understanding of the most critical problems facing small business in general and the minority entrepreneur in particular. Analyzing the story in terms of the previously-cited SBA list of handicaps faced by small businesses, we can see that McClellan's clients came up short on a number of points:

1. There was some lack of business know-how.
2. There was some lack of individual qualifications.
3. The business was effectively undercapitalized; it was unable to respond to an emergency that, although brought on by mismanagement, was an emergency nonetheless.
4. Given the abrupt product changeover, the business may well have been marginal in the first place.

Where Are All the Qualified People?

McClellan's story leads us inevitably to an examination of another problem dogging those who would create minority businesses: Where do you find the trained experienced minority managers to run them? This is a complicated issue, with tangled and snarled social, cultural, and economic roots. It derives in part from generations of overt and covert discrimination that has separated minorities from the economic mainstream and deprived them not only of a vibrant business heritage, but also of successful practitioners to serve as examples. It derives from poor schools and poor quality education. It derives from misplaced emphasis in both public and private programs for training the disadvantaged. It derives from an absence of true mobility and promotional opportunity for those minority citizens who do make it into our corporations. It derives . . . but the reader can probably supply his own additions to this sketchy list.

The point is that, as Dr. Brimmer has already pointed out, there is probably an inadequate pool of qualified minority managerial talent to take profitable advantage of the few opportunities that do exist. This shortage would seem to translate about the same way when the opportunity is on the assembly line, at the keypunch, or in front of the "GO" button on the computer.

Says Robert Edelen, recalling his conversation with our respondents, "Many of the firms that were interested in hiring blacks found that there were an insufficient number of them adequately trained in the business skills that were needed. They had not obtained this training either through formal education or experience. . . . An examination of the varieties of educational programs that are supposed to turn out trained, ready-to-function minority administrators simply are not doing this. Minority businessmen need to be introduced to business training if they are to succeed, but those in charge have not yet developed the effort necessary to achieve this end."

Agencies like ICBO and SBA have ambitious programs to provide business counseling to active and hopeful minority entrepreneurs. But there is evidence that their activities, taken in sum with those of the other agencies, are simply unequal to the task. Chad McClellan has had a ringside view of the problem and he concedes, "Frankly, the talent of the order needed apparently is not available in just the Negro community alone." At the time of his interview, McClellan was trying to put together a South Central Los Angeles business with a potential volume of $600,000 a year.

"We think there is a promise for putting together black and white entrepreneurs who have a common interest and common purpose," he said. "We can find the money, but we are also looking for management, people qualified to go in there and run it and willing to put some of their own money on the line. . . . It is tough going. We haven't been able to do it yet. This is a dilemma. This is the kind of frustrating problem we have."

In spite of difficulties, McClellan is openly optimistic. He praises ICBO's efforts in providing advice and counsel to minority businessmen. With pardonable pride, he points to the success of his own efforts in convincing corporations to recruit, hire, promote, and train minority workers. (Appendix A summarizes a University of Southern California study on employer experience with minority employees.) He also is interested in the Peder Corporation's program to counsel minority middle managers who have become stalled in their careers.

On the general subject of minority jobs, McClellan says, "No company should hire anyone it doesn't need. But if there is a place for a minority employee, then it is wise to give him a somewhat better-than-average chance to succeed. If he isn't qualified, or if he needs other kinds of help to be able to perform the job, then he should get that kind of help."

Where? McClellan looks to the creation of "skill centers of some type that can certify that persons are qualified for jobs to which they have been referred." But he would expect the centers to provide basic literacy instruction and attitudinal counseling as well. Above all, these centers must not be ends in themselves, preparing their students for jobs that are marginal or will soon become obsolete. They must provide the kind of experience that leads to long-term employment. (Appendix B describes the work of the Urban League Data Processing Training Center, a skill center whose placement record has been encouraging.)

The Will to Succeed

"Frankly, I'm not nearly so excited about minority capitalism as I am about all citizens having a vision of the opportunity that springs from enterprise," says Chad McClellan. He adds that the complete answer to economic emergence of minority populations may well go beyond programs that stress jobs and minority ownership.

"The answer is to be found in motivation," he says with conviction. "And motivation is only stimulated by the incentive that springs from ultimate success. I don't care what your color is, if you aren't motivated you aren't going to succeed. Whatever means we can find to give the black man or Mexican-American a vision of opportunity, then that means is the best way I know to generate motivation."

Unfortunately, the kinds of successful business examples that might inspire motivation are virtually nonexistent in our study. But the problem reaches much deeper. On the whole, minority business has traditionally been small business, but small business of the marginal "Mom-and-Pop" variety. A study of several such operations, described in a later chapter, shows that the proprietors are far too preoccupied with merely surviving from one day to the next to worry about planning, expansion, and whatever responsibility they might have for serving as community success models. Just as poverty and race are becoming ever more entwined, so are small business and minority business. Unless assistance programs recognize this fact, both the latter may end like San Francisco's celebrated cable cars—expensive to operate, quaint, hopelessly anachronistic to meet the needs of the times. Should such a fate overtake minority business, then a valuable beacon of hope for minorities will be extinguished.

RACE, RACE, RACE—
LOCATION, LOCATION, LOCATION

In pondering ways to broaden the basis of minority participation in economic activity, the planner cannot sidestep the symbiosis of poverty and race. Unlike symbiosis in the life sciences, however, this variety is both painful and debilitating. It creates a vicious cycle in which the two elements feed upon each other.

By any yardstick, South Central and East Los Angeles rate far below the rest of the region in terms of income, education, employment and employment potential, and housing quality. East Los Angeles is predominantly Mexican-American; South Central is largely black. Intuitively, one would expect disproportionate difficulties in attempting to establish new businesses in either section. And the study findings bear this out.

Economic conditions in both areas militate against long-term profitability for the kinds of marginal operations associated up to now with ghetto neighborhoods. To put it bluntly, regardless of the weight of commitment to social causes, businesses face a risky future when they must depend primarily or exclusively upon minority markets. Such markets offer only limited profit potential, creating a situation in which the new business, no matter how well-intentioned or well-financed, seems doomed to a marginal future.

Although several of the Los Angeles assistance agencies seek to get around this fact by imposing standards for scale of operations or profit potential, the results have been less than encouraging.

Jobs Versus Business Ownership

Given the uncertainty that minority capitalism can take hold, prosper, and rejuvenate the central city, the issue of creating jobs assumes much greater significance. In the disadvantaged areas of Los Angeles, our own and other studies show that the demand for jobs far outruns the supply. Moreover, those who do need work are usually too poor to move nearer to job sources—not to mention the still troublesome problem of racial discrimination in housing. To make the impasse complete, there is inadequate public transportation to and from major places of employment and the inner city.

Clearly, then, the only answer lies—at least for the time being—in locating branches of the major employers in disadvantaged areas. However, such a move must clearly be tied to job training to assure a supply of qualified manpower. And the whole effort must be coordinated and accompanied by business commitment, lest expensive job development and training programs be undertaken only to prove wasteful and disillusioning when business reconsiders and the openings fail to materialize.

A recent report by the Federal Reserve Bank of San Francisco took the following view of the jobs-versus-ownership question:

> Job skills and an attendant earning power are presumably more important to the ghetto resident than the location of his job, and the mere injection of capital to create minority-owned businesses where there are no complementary resources is not likely to revitalize the urban slums on anything approaching a lasting basis.
>
> In order to survive, the minority businessman must, above all, make profits. Making profits is a prerequisite to making employment for his minority neighbors. Otherwise, black capitalism could easily become synonymous with the situation of marginal profits, bankruptcy and attendant disillusionment.
>
> Even if the number of minority entrepreneurs were to be vastly expanded, moreover, the aggregate effect upon unemployment and income in the ghetto areas probably would not be very great. Indeed, a two percent increase in employment and wages of ghetto residents could well have a much greater effect upon the over-all quality of urban life than would a 100 percent increase in the numbers and profits of minority entrepreneurs.[3]

When it comes to relying on corporations to furnish the impetus for job expansion, however, our gadfly, Robert Edelen, is typically suspicious. Because the major companies operating in central Los Angeles are not minority-owned enterprises, they represent a special kind of activity not dealt with in detail in this study. Nevertheless, they came up often enough in interviews for Edelen to form a few opinions.

"They are in the inner city primarily because of capital investments by the parent company and federal grants they lobbied for to support training programs," Edelen says. "Although the money officially goes into training and educating minorities for various kinds of responsibilities in the business world, much of what has been done appears inadequate for the kinds of jobs the trainees have been promised."

Edelen charges that some of the corporations simply use their inner-city subsidiary operations to generate losses that can be used as write-offs against profits made on other contracts. "If this is correct," he says, "then it is fair to ask if the parent companies are really interested in producing good profits from their subsidiary operations. Even though some of these subsidiaries are managed by black men with executive titles, the managers express a certain anger and disgust with the way the programs are running. They stay on because it's the one place they can bring down $20-25,000 a year and earn a good living for their families."

TO RECAPITULATE

What have we discovered so far about our subject, this phenomenon called minority capitalism? First of all, despite a very favorable treatment by the news media, it has come under a cloud of suspicion, not only from academic skeptics, but also from an increasing number of practitioners.

The reason is the nature of the problems involved. They are not the kind that a minor course correction can alleviate. They are fundamental, lying far below the surface and directly related to the core issue of whether minority capitalism is either economically or socially feasible. While the reader might challenge Robert Edelen's perception of the situation, and even reject outright his outspokenly pessimistic evaluation of the programs, we are convinced of both the reality and persistence of these problems. In an informed, but relatively unsophisticated way, Edelen is raising the same issues detailed in more scholarly reports published by various agencies and foundations.

The next chapter will deal with these issues through the eyes of practicing minority entrepreneurs. They will speak to us about their quest for capital, about costly delays in fulfilling administrative and bureaucratic requirements, about the shortage of experienced managerial and technical help, about motivation and about lingering vestiges of racial discrimination against minority businessmen.

Our method here was the personal interview, by which we were able to compile a number of real-life case histories. Naturally, they are subjective, and in this sense, they must be weighed as carefully as Robert Edelen's commentary. But it was the practical Dr. Johnson who cautioned, "The use of traveling is to regulate imagination by reality, and instead of thinking how things may be, to see them as they are." Let us travel then.

NOTES

1. Andrew F. Brimmer and Henry S. Terrell, "The Economic Potential of Black Capitalism," paper given at 82nd meeting of the American Economic Association, New York, 1969.

2. Robert K. Otterbourg, "Which Route for Blacks in Business?" *Wall Street Journal*, July 10, 1970, p. 6.

3. Verle Johnston, "Financing the Inner City," *Monthly Review*, Federal Reserve Bank of San Francisco, October 1969, p. 210.

4

THE VIEW
FROM
THE TRENCHES

Eleven minority enterprises. They might sell you a book or a bonbon, pasta or a pill, a mattress or a magazine rack. If you wished to publish a song, you could buy the paper from one company and the printing services from another. Assuming your song were to be recorded, a third company might sell you a portable stereo record player. Such commercial success would allow you to indulge your fondest career ambitions, in which case yet another firm could sell you a pool table and a sandbox. Then the remaining firm in our sample could cement your new status by featuring you in a *cinema-verité* production for public television.

If our respondent firms seem to have little in common when it comes to their products, they compensate by presenting marked similarities in their problems. Not surprisingly, the biggest single problem is money, or rather the lack of money to advertise, or expand, or innovate, or do any of the things that enables a small business to turn the magic corner toward solvency and permanence. Adequate capitalization is the most tantalizing rainbow of all to the entrepreneurs in our study—more so than management training, business counseling, a pool of experienced workers, nondiscrimination, preferential government programs, or even ethnic pride.

A DOLLAR IS A DOLLAR IS A DOLLAR

"I believe that most small businesses, in particular the small black businesses with which I'm most familiar, start out undercapitalized," said a young black who started his own paper products business about a year before the interview. "Minority businessmen won't ask bankers for $5,000 to cover advertising, because they're afraid the answer is going to be 'no.' But they need advertising to build up sales. I'll be the first to admit that the problems of minority business are many. But usually, they start out with too little capital."

The result is that the Los Angeles minority entrepreneur simply has little or no financial cushion if his market goes sour, or there is a credit crunch, or he makes mistakes in judgment. "I think you have to learn to live with the fact that you are virtually bankrupt all the time," said an electronics expert who developed what he believes to be a totally new design concept for stereo record players. "If you want to start a business, you have to make up your mind to spend, spend, spend. It isn't easy to do, with money so hard to come by, but you can't hold back. You can find assistance on making the decisions, yes. But you have to do things yourself."

Undercapitalization sets in motion a chain of discouraging business circumstances. The manager of a wood products firm spoke for many in our sample when he lamented, "We're experiencing a severe capital problem that keeps us from increasing sales, that keeps us from earning higher profits. Frankly, the financial climate just isn't favorable to raising money for minority businesses—or any business except the giants, for that matter. Money for us is about as tight as it has ever been. The banks won't move one step without a government guarantee."

The manager of a macaroni factory agreed completely. "Adequate capital?" he echoes, the irony in his voice unmistakable. "We operate strictly out of cash flow . . . from hand to mouth. If we run into any difficulties today, we can literally be out of business tomorrow. We don't have a net worth. We are a typical minority company operating by the seat of its pants. Very typical."

An East Los Angeles mattress plant, built largely on Chicano hopes and a $10,000 loan from a foundation, borrowed a tactic from the street people in dealing with the problem of short capital. "Our solution was simple," said a spokesman. "Hustle. Looking for an edge. We learned that in the dominant society people get rich by making other people's money work for them. So we put our $10,000 in local banks and used it as collateral for equipment purchases. In effect we took our $10,000 damned near to $15,000 this way." He admitted, however, that his operation was chronically underfinanced.

A woodworker who wanted to expand his well-established and profitable business found that the agencies drove a hard bargain and took an inordinately long time to make up their minds. "They kept me on the hook for months," he said, "and the time away from the shop was hurting the business." He finally decided to do what several entrepreneurs in the sample had to do—go it alone. "I'll secure the loan with my own personal and real property. Everything, present and future, will be tied up. I know I won't have a leg to stand on if a contract falls through or I hit a rough spot somewhere else. It really doesn't seem fair." He had been in the woodworking business over 40 years.

IN THE BEGINNING WAS . . .

In a later chapter, the reader will encounter a minority businessman who awoke one day and found himself the proprietor of a cleaning products business—an outright gift from a neighbor. The subjects of the present chapter were not so lucky. They had to scratch to get launched, and scratch hard.

Our aspiring Chicano mattress-makers took their proposal to the Mexican American Community Foundation, an offspring of the giant Ford Foundation. They received $10,000 interest free, repayable over the next two years. It was as welcome as a smogless day in Los Angeles, although still some $10,000 short of what they felt was needed.

A printing company that was limping painfully went another route to find its transfusion of funds. The owners approached the top management of one of the country's leading systems engineering corporations and asked for help. The corporate officers not only agreed to contribute money but also detached one of their own managers "to make managerial and technical inputs" and, in effect, run the business. Then the corporation placed a few sizable orders for printing.

Two partners who founded a bookstore did it by looking inward to their own resources, both financial and managerial. "Getting started is the easiest thing in the world if you're willing to work five to ten years, not take salary and turn the profits back to the business," one of the partners stated, only half-facetiously. The two began their association while each held a full-time job elsewhere. One opened the store in the morning, the other closed in the evening, and family members manned the cash registers during the day. It was a gruelling and drawn-out process that finally paid off.

Was it absolutely necessary? "It's the way you finance business if you're a black man," the other partner insists. "The minute you tell a lending institution you're a minority business, you put yourself in a risk category where those people won't carry you over a bail-out period. They're out to make a profit off sounder investments."

Self-capitalization was the path followed by the woodworker we spoke of earlier. He simply came home from his job, spent the evening in his shop, and turned all the profits back into his business. As we shall see later, this procedure worked well until he needed money to expand. The same was true of the candy manufacturers in our sample. They began on a shoestring, worked several years to get on their feet, and ran into trouble when it came time to finance growth.

Syndication and some donated obsolete machinery were the elements that put our macaroni manufacturer in motion. Fourteen black financiers provided the seed money after a rail company had given them some aging equipment. As an opportunity, it may have been less than ideal. Says the company manager, "The whole thing was a sham perpetrated on the black community and black investors . . . I wouldn't have put a quarter into it. We have 40-year-old equipment. Spending $180,000 to refurbish it is like spending money to refurbish a 1939 Hudson."

The experience of the inventor who came up with a better stereo record player is neater and doubtless more appealing to those who prefer a text-book flavor to their business histories. As he says: "Incorporation seemed the best way to generate capital, and I talked to a number of people. Money as a problem was secondary to control—who could run the company.

"When we incorporated, we had authorization for $100,000 capitalization," he goes on. "Several people came in, for a total of $29,000, and I retained 70 percent of the stock in exchange for my patent rights. I am now both majority stockholder and president and chairman of the board of the corporation."

Our last entrepreneur in this section took stock of himself and decided that although he was a trained and experienced chemist, he fell short of the financial and managerial resources necessary to launch a pharmaceutical manufacturing concern. His remedy was to approach a prominent—and large—corporation in the pharmaceutical field to obtain financing for a home-grown business, his own, that would appeal directly to the minority community. The combination of his own experience and the potential for capitalizing on emerging minority consciousness proved effective. The company came in. As we shall see, however, the management expertise did not.

At the time, though, there appeared to be several advantages, chief among which were marketing and administrative assistance, better insurance rates and coverage, lower leasing rates for automobiles, and a more favorable line of credit. (Our chemist, by the way, was unaware that the Small Business Administration offered management assistance.) Not all was ideal, however. For example, the break-even deadline in the financing agreement proved unrealistically short. There was no immediate equity for the management team, although such participation was to become available through stock options when the enterprise went public shortly after the break-even point.

AND WHAT ABOUT THE AGENCIES?

So far we have said nothing of the well-publicized private and governmental programs expressly designed to finance the creation of minority businesses. But a number of respondents did approach one or another of these agencies for initial financing. Not all shared the opinion of our pharmaceutical manufacturer that "the masses of paperwork and the resulting length of time necessary to get into the marketplace made me look at SBA as a last resort."

In the beginning at least, the stereo inventor had no such second thoughts about SBA. Later, however, the track record made him reassess his thinking. He sought a guaranteed 90-percent loan from SBA for purchase of a 27,000-square-foot factory in Compton. At the time of original SBA authorization, the prime rate was 5.5 percent. But delays were such that by the time the money was to be granted, the contract called for a five-year loan at eight percent. To make matters even worse, the bank had second thoughts and decided to lend only $41,500 of the $350,000 originally agreed upon.

A stereo expert complained, "There was a cash flow analysis by Peat, Marwick, Mitchell & Co., and a feasibility study by the Department of Commerce. But the bank was unimpressed and totally disregarded the fact that we were right in the middle of setting up the facility and getting going. You bet your life we screamed bloody murder about them backing down."

The upshot of all this was increased stock authorization to raise $100,000 in new equity financing. The inventor saw his 70 percent of shares outstanding shrink to 55 percent. "We found out," he recalls somewhat ruefully, "that SBA is powerless with a bank. The bank's position with SBA on these kinds of loans favors the bank. There are no government teeth in this kind of loan situation."

The Chicano mattress-maker found that increased lender awareness of minority needs and problems made it a fairly easy matter to get into the loan manager's office and receive a sympathetic audience. But perhaps the first lesson he and his colleagues learned is that favorable or special handling of minority borrowers is the stuff of publicity releases. "The criteria for getting a loan are the same now as they've always been," he reports. "Credit . . . personal credibility . . . the whole bit. The things that have traditionally excluded the minority guy who's down and out are still there."

They may be, but there are other ways. The printing company in the sample applied through SBA, ERC, and to several banks without success. The minute their guardian angel, the systems engineering corporation, stepped into the picture as a guarantor, however, the entire picture changed. The printers promptly received a sizable loan from a private bank. Moreover, the unfavorable experience with SBA did not sour the firm, which is aggressively pursuing contracts under the agency's 8A program.

Less Woe But Not Woeless

Some companies fared better than others in their dealings with the agencies. None, however, escaped without at least a little emotional damage. "We were almost to our wits' end before approval finally came through," said the manager of the wood products firm as he recalled the general anxiety over an SBA loan. He still shuddered at the "many, many" delays and numerous revisions and updatings required in processing his firm's $450,000 loan application under the agency's 90-percent guarantee plan.

A six-month delay in getting the money was particularly vexing in this case, since a large share of the proceeds was earmarked for operating expenses. Still, the experience could not have been entirely intimidating. At the time of our survey, the company was involved with SBIC and SBA in negotiating two new loans.

The SBA program also benefited our macaroni manufacturer to the tune of $250,000, but only after "eight months of going in, going out, being very persistent and staying right there with them." This kind of incessant pressure was necessary, he explains, because the agency was, "to put it politely, reluctant to provide the loan." Since $180,000 went into renovating equipment, and a good share of the remainder into operating expenses, little was left to develop a market for the product. The firm lives a precarious existence on government contracts.

An enterprising young black who founded his own paper products business invested $22,500 in personal funds and approached SBA for the remainder of the $150,000 that he considered essential to get started. "They were moving much too slowly," he recalls, "so I went to ERC in hopes of keeping to the development schedule I'd set up." His turned out to be one of the first organizations backed by ERC—the loan was $130,000.

One that ERC did not back was a candy manufacturer grossing about $250,000 annually. The husband-wife owners approached banks, SBA, and

ERC, each time with a notable lack of success. They expected to use the loan to buy in larger quantities, enjoy a substantial discount, and realize higher profits from gross sales. This, in turn, would have enabled them (in theory) to penetrate new markets beyond the churches, welfare groups, and boys' clubs that contributed the lion's share of their business.

In a sample full of disappointments, one experience stood apart. It began promisingly enough when the proprietor of the woodworking shop approached ERC for assistance in putting together a proposal for funds to acquire a new building. ERC steered the applicant to *Impact* which in turn helped complete the proposal and locate a satisfactory property at "quite reasonable" terms. Then the problems began.

At the time of this survey the proposal had been bouncing back and forth between the bank and SBA "for six or seven months." The respondent was vague about the origin of his difficulties and how to go about reconciling them with either the lender or the agency. His surest opinion was that the paperwork was poorly executed—"not the right forms and stuff like that." He insisted he was spending so much time trying to right the situation that his business was suffering.

"Sometimes I get the feeling that I don't know what I'm doing," he confessed. "And they act like they're giving me the money instead of me paying 9.5 percent. I've been trying to get some of the money allocated for small business at 5.5 or 6 percent, but I can't seem to find where it is." (At this point in the interview, the respondent received a call from the bank requesting a current financial statement. His had been current 90 days before when he resubmitted the application.)

In desperation he had collected letters from some of his oldest customers, one of whom guaranteed him business at a level of about $400,000 a year. "That one letter turned out to be detrimental to my cause," he lamented, "because the bank then told me I was depending too much on one customer. Instead of helping me, it hindered me." Meanwhile, this customer was being held up by the respondent's lack of capital to expand enough to do the work. "I've been promised so often by SBA that I'm not going to depend on them any more," he sighed.

Our last voice in this sequence belongs to a young film-maker who came up against the SBA's edict against lending to any enterprise with a potential for propagandizing—film-making, publishing, broadcasting, and the like. Unfortunately for him and his partners, they were well along in preparing their proposal for SBA when this unfortunate fact was brought to their attention. At that point, as he says, someone in the agency suggested they reapply to open a barbershop or barbecue stand. His attitude was one of bafflement. "If I wanted to go into manufacturing, I could probably get backing from SBA. Then I could take my profits and propagandize." The distinction seemed to escape him.

SOME RESIDUE OF BITTERNESS

Although the film-maker spoke calmly, the resignation in his voice was tinged with bitterness. Others spoke more bluntly. Said the pharmaceutical manufacturer, "The federal government is only going to develop cobbler shops or cafés or that kind of thing that will net at the most $50,000 to $100,000 a year. To me that is a far cry from putting the minority businessman into the mainstream."

The bookstore owner was even more caustic. "Minority capitalism is one of the biggest frauds ever perpetrated on the aspirations of the black people," he declared. "They're pork barrels for politicians to use for putting their people in jobs. We had four projections turned down by SBA. The last time we took it to a major investment company. Their representative laughed and asked, 'How could they possibly turn this down.' We looked for other routes."

Our candy-maker said flatly that any minority entrepreneur should expect to make his way on his own with no help from anyone. He insisted that he could only have received assistance from SBA by paying from $200 to $2,000 or from ERC only at the risk of losing control of his business. "It seems to me there is really no plan or intention to develop minority business so I don't waste my time any more with these so-called helping agencies. I hope to save enough money on my own to expand the business."

Not everyone was so disillusioned. The manager of the wood products firm chided SBA on its lack of aggressiveness in seeking out promising candidates for economic assistance, but added this softening observation: "Dumping money into a company without a reasonable chance for success is nothing short of fiscal foolishness. It leaves a sour taste with Congress and the taxpayers and makes the road just that much more difficult for the really able guy who can make a go of it."

HOW ABOUT EDUCATIONAL PROGRAMS AMONG THE AGENCIES? HOW ABOUT TECHNICAL ASSISTANCE?

Operating on the persuasive theory that it takes both money and management expertise to bring a business enterprise to success, the agencies under scrutiny in this study provide a variety of training and counseling programs. Our mattress-maker was not overly impressed with what SBA had to offer. "SBA has management classes, but how do they use them," he asked. "They teach general things, not the solutions to problems individuals will have to solve in business. And this is what is needed. But the government doesn't give that kind of course."

Disappointment also marked the experience of our wood products firm in obtaining managerial assistance. The manager got in touch with SBA Service Corps of Retired Executives (SCORE), but nothing definite emerged. His association with ICBO was more productive, however, and he reported good results from that agency's work in setting up loan applications and contracts.

ICBO also came in for a share of praise from the stereo inventor who spent a year working with an ICBO advisor in developing market plans for his record player. He was enthusiastic not only about the strategy of assigning seasoned businessmen on a one-to-one basis, but also about the real effort made to match backgrounds and, to the extent possible, personalities.

"It isn't just a matter of finding someone to give advice," he explained, "it's finding the right someone . . . a person who can cut past your egotism and get to the realities." The inventor's alter ego in this case was a highly experienced, retired businessman. "He encouraged me, yes," the entrepreneur said, "but he could be tough, too, and ask the hard-nosed questions and demand the hard-nosed decisions."

In general, his ICBO experience convinced our inventor that the ICBO style of intermediary is a workable way to get minority capitalism off the ground. He felt that a potential entrepreneur, however gifted, was failure-prone without help in developing a long-range plan and technical aid in implementing it. He took strong exception to those programs that offered money without the kind of consulting assistance available through ICBO. Such programs he labeled "rudderless" and "instant failures."

Our woodworker, who experienced such severe problems with the agencies in arranging financing, fared little better in obtaining counseling services. Some three years before the interview he had tried ICBO with no results. At the time of the interview, he was having difficulty in working through *Impact* to set up his books and locate full-time bookkeeping assistance. At one point, he was visited by a representative of a national accounting firm who announced his readiness to begin work for "about $1,500." This was about $1,500 more than the free service the woodworker says he had been told to expect, and he backed off. He was still waiting.

THE NEED IS THERE, HOWEVER

Although most respondents agreed that management training and assistance are only part of what is required to make minority capitalism a living reality, they were in virtual unanimity that these services are exceeded in importance only by the need for adequate financing. Let us now look at some actual operating experiences where lack of training or counseling proved costly. In each case, the entrepreneur felt the problem could have been avoided through timely advice. None was forthcoming.

On moving into the pharmaceutical field in Los Angeles, our manufacturer chose to go with proprietary lines whose appearance would be spearheaded by a hard-hitting advertising campaign in the minority community. Seven products were offered, solely through retail outlets. Sales proved so disappointing that it was decided to scrap some of the products and improve the selection by adding ethical lines marketed to a select group of black physicians.

By the time this decision was made, however, the damage had been done. The advertising budget was depleted, and the results had been negligible. Part of the failure was due to a mistake in judgment that had led the firm into competing head-on with well-advertised national brands. Also, the management overrated the sales potential of its retail outlets and realized too late that the largest volume is done in chain-store operations which are difficult to crack.

After two quarters, it was necessary to return to the parent company for additional capital. Advertising was cut back, and the entire market strategy overhauled. All this could have been avoided, the manager feels, if reliable market counseling had been available. As it was, the firm had to reassess its position, identify its true market, obtain additional capital, and radically change its product lines.

Imperfect market analysis was demonstrated even more dramatically in the early days of our wood products company. The first product was a baseball bat made of ash, a superior wood for this use. However, it was only after the firm went into production that the management learned of the scarcity of supplies of ash. It became impossible to meet manufacturing schedules, and the bat was dropped. The impact was both financial and psychological. Recovery came slowly through the introduction of a wider line of wood products, offered through retail stores both inside and outside the minority community.

Lack of expertise continued to plague the macaroni company. Its manager lamented that the business got started before its principals realized they did not have access to anyone who knew either the production or marketing side of the business. The manager learned by reading and trial-and-error. He reached all the way to the Philippines to find his plant manager and brought in experts who knew how to set up a production operation. Even with this, the macaroni had yet to be accepted for the consumer market. Certain government agencies were the only customers.

The owner of the paper supply house got into difficulty because "being young, I was overzealous, unseasoned, and took a lot of things for granted." He acted on promises of business, bought equipment, and suffered a sharp departure from projected cash flow when some of the promises failed to materialize. This led to a minor credit problem on the one hand, but, more seriously, it caused him to negotiate poor terms with lenders who also believed his over-ambitious cash-flow analysis. Soon he found himself in violation of some agreements, and it took time from the business to set matters right. A knowledgeable advisor at the outset would have been invaluable.

WHENCE COMETH THE EXPERTISE?—A SUBJECTIVE VIEW

"We have to utilize the expertise of others . . . We have to stop being afraid of each other," declared the manager of the macaroni factory. "You have to surround yourself with capable people who know what they're doing. A businessman must rely on the brains of other people that he can control. Failing to do this is to me the biggest downfall in any business."

Asked how he would create a pool of this kind of talent in the minority community, the manager put his faith in practical on-the-job experience. "They just have to roll up their sleeves and get their hands dirty," he said. "And they have to be more forceful—with lenders, in selling, with suppliers. They have to know what they want and not let anything sidetrack them from getting it. Why, I'd recruit a gorilla if that was the only way to get this job done."

The young paper supplier cited two chief ways to acquire the needed experience. "The biggest failure is not knowing management, and black businesses in particular will not admit this weakness. One way to overcome it is the traditional route through college to apprenticeship in a large corporation. And you know, this isn't open to many blacks. The other alternative is to get in there and do it. Then you have to be a bastard, you have to be offensive and tenacious. Most of all you have to die hard because there are many points along the way where dying can be quite easy. The second biggest failure, I believe, is in not being aggressive enough."

Our bookstore manager saw the problem as one in human relations and said bluntly that the minority community would have to overcome itself before real progress would be made. "My association with black businessmen and executives has been a great disappointment," he said. "We haven't gotten past that ego stage to where we really want to do something. We don't have the humility to let go of this status thing and make room for those who are qualified to move through.

"The black executive must get rid of this ego hang-up and get down in his community and start setting an example for the young. It's that sapling who's coming up that we must go and direct—and not at arm's length either. We've got to sit down and let him see and feel and learn that we're human, that if he applies himself he can do anything we can do. To me, that's the black businessman's highest role . . . setting an example for the young."

"WELL, I THINK 'THEY' OUGHT TO . . . "

Our businessmen are not without opinions—strong opinions—about what private business, government, and education can do to strengthen and extend the concept of minority capitalism. There are also a few opinions on the responsibilities of the minority community toward itself. The reader should always bear in mind that these views are the products of trying, often with dismaying lack of success, to make a small minority enterprise viable. In many cases, the attitudes were forged in disappointment and tempered with disenchantment.

"We have to strike out after some of the larger, more general markets," said the manager of the mattress factory, bemoaning the fact that his principal customers were welfare agencies in the Chicano community. He felt that his product was gaining a reputation for quality outside the minority area and the time to move was ripe. He hoped the SBA set-aside program (8A) would be the vehicle to put expansion in motion. But he was dubious.

"Their definition of 'small business' is anyone who doesn't do over a million dollars in sales—yearly average," he said. "Well, to us that's not small business. That's big business. And we can't compete against somebody like that with our capital, that is, somebody who's got $900,000 in sales a year and 300 employees. We just can't come up with a competitive price ticket. Even if we did, that other businessman would be able to undercut us. So we're after the government to re-evaluate the set-aside program and establish new categories for companies like ours. Until this is done, we have to say, 'You're not really helping us.' "

The wood products company manager believed that more diversified management experience is an essential key to the future of minority capitalism. "Historically," he pointed out, "minorities have done better and been found in larger numbers in corporations. But there they tend to specialize. They seldom get the broad exposure I feel is necessary in running your own business. You almost have to be in a fairly small business to gain this diversity of experience. Courses in business administration can help—I've profited from some—but again there is only so much you can learn from a textbook."

Our stereo inventor would begin by reforming the relationship between government and private banks. "As great as it is in concept," he said, "the SBA loan program is toothless. Banks should be required to lend money in every case where the government agrees to guarantee. After all, there's no risk to the bank or its depositors. And SBA should be able to enforce sanctions against any bank that doesn't honor its obligation. I know of cases where people didn't survive, because the bank unilaterally changed its mind. It almost happened to us."

Hard Knocks Do Serve a Useful Purpose

All this is not to say that our respondents want a situation where everything is designed to shield the minority entrepreneur from the realities of competition in the business world. They are quick to point out that this would ultimately prove counterproductive.

"I really don't think there is any shortcut to success," said the inventor. "It's probably necessary over the long haul to experience all the problems, take the gambles, make the mistakes. It's a learning situation where you get burned a few times and either acquire the wisdom or pass from the scene. It would be nice to have a lot of financing, but that usually means you lose control. And the whole thing in this minority capitalism idea is to place the minority businessman in control of his own destiny."

The young proprietor of our paper products firm agreed wholeheartedly with the notion of developing strength and toughness through struggle. "You learn to struggle, and you grow stronger and more honest about your own strengths and weaknesses," he stated. "It's not a thing you learn from a book; institutional education right down to the nitty-gritty. You give it all you've got. How else can I tell you?"

Private Enterprise as a Resource

In general our respondents placed a great deal of confidence—and expectation—in private industry as a force to make minority capitalism the breakthrough that its exponents hope it will be. Said the pharmaceutical manager, "My personal feeling is that private enterprise, particularly the large companies, is the one that will have to supply the impetus. It has the wealth of experience to guide the minority businessman, the manpower to assist him in making his day-to-day operating decisions. They've been there and they know all the angles. Without the support of private enterprise, I don't think minorities will ever get into the mainstream of business or industry."

The owner of the paper products company felt that private businesses could help in two very practical ways. First, they could furnish support in the form of orders. He maintained that his firm could furnish both faster and more economical service on certain smaller jobs than his larger competitors. His view was that in awarding their contracts customers should give special consideration to this kind of flexibility and to the altruistic rewards of assisting minority business.

The second practical boost would be for "big business" to be much more dependable about paying its bills on time. "When you're a small businessman," he said, "you can't afford to have the giants playing and working on your money. You must be able to collect your receivables rapidly and convert your payables even faster. Many of the larger companies are the worst offenders about being late in their payments. Their excuses don't pay the bills of small business."

A common attitude among many respondents was the feeling that large businesses could do a lot more to tutor minority youngsters in the amenities of getting ahead in the business world. Our bookstore owner probably put it as well as anyone. "Industry must explain to the young minority applicant why it is necessary to be a man of dignity and character and to be polite," he urged. "Many young blacks approach business as they'd approach visitors from another world, and to my way of thinking, business has a responsibility to help them overcome their doubts and defensiveness."

The young film-maker recommended that private enterprise develop a higher degree of color blindness in its credit dealings with minority businessmen. He backed off from labeling minority credit problems a result of discrimination, and chalked it up instead to "like helps like . . . we see it all the time." He said he experienced unrelieved failure in trying to borrow money, while white film-makers, in circumstances nearly identical with his own, had little difficulty attracting financing.

Government as a Resource

SBA's 8A program was viewed by our paper products entrepreneur as a leading example of the right kind of help government should extend to the struggling minority businessman. He had recently won a $70,000 contract under the program and was understandably enthusiastic. "With what is really a small investment," he said, "SBA and the General Services Administration were able to help a small business stay alive and function at a competitive level."

He would like to see 8A expanded to embrace more minority firms and a higher volume of government purchases. In addition, he felt there was considerable virtue in government programs designed to compensate employers for on-the-job training of the unskilled. His own experience under such arrangements had been "very satisfactory."

In general, our respondents agreed that government could be most useful in these ways: speeding up the loan approval process and exerting more pressure on banks to take risks; giving preferential treatment to minority firms on government contracts; providing counseling and formal training courses; authorizing payment (supplementary) for employing the unskilled and providing on-the-job training; establishing government scholarships for qualified minority students who want to study for a business career.

DISCRIMINATION

Predictably, the subject of discrimination came up repeatedly in the interviews. There was remarkably little bitterness, considering that many of the respondents were veteran businessmen who had been struggling for success and recognition many years before discrimination became the national issue it is today. Let us hear what they have to say.

Our printing shop manager had looked far and wide without success for a black shop foreman. "There isn't one in the United States," he concluded, "simply because discrimination—particularly by the union—has prevented the black man from gaining this experience. In fact, there is a critical shortage of experienced minority business operators in all fields as a result of years and years of discrimination. Today it doesn't seem an insurmountable problem, but its past effects are a serious hindrance to the success of minority business."

This vacuum seems to produce a side-effect when minority entrepreneurs approach lenders. "Let's face it," said the candy-maker, "the banks I have to approach don't do business with minority manufacturers, because there are none. When I announce that I'm going into the mainstream of business, they mentally click off the few statistics they have on failure rates. They say, 'Wow, how do we know this guy can do what he says he can do.' And even if they're sincerely motivated to help, or are under pressure from the SBA, they are lukewarm at the most from a business point of view. It wouldn't be that way if I were white.

"I know how it goes," he continued. "They compare me with what they've seen before—mostly café owners and barbershop operators. I'm a rarity that they don't quite know how to handle. But they'll lend to a white businessman who wants to get into the same market. It doesn't even matter if he has failed in a business before, or even if he sank a company. He's white and that's their image of a businessman. A prototype and a stereotype."

The bookstore owner draws some unusual distinctions between discrimination as practiced in the South and North (or West). "To me, the Northerner is more deadly to the minority businessman than the white Southerner. The Southerner has lived around blacks, knows them, and isn't afraid of them. But the Northerner is isolated in his own suburban ghetto and only knows what he reads in his newspaper or sees on television. There is no identification or understanding.

"So how does this work in business? When I finally get to meet a third-line officer in a little branch bank, I can almost see him saying to himself,

'Well, boy, what do you want.' Outwardly he's his crisp polite Northern self, but inwardly he projects that same hard-nosed line we mistakenly say is common only to white Southerners.

"At least the Southern white is honest. He'll say, 'If you come in here, here's what you have to do' or 'Take it and go 'way over there and sell it.' But the Northerner tells you, 'This is my market and you have no right to enter it. We don't want anything to do with you.' And California is no more liberal in this attitude than anywhere else, regardless of its reputation."

At the macaroni factory, discrimination seemed to operate primarily against technical assistance. "We couldn't get any," said the manager, "once people found out the business was all black and there was no white around to advise us. People in the industry wouldn't touch us with a ten-foot pole. We had four engineering firms out here, but they took one look at our 40-year-old equipment and ran like bandits. It boiled down to the point where the banks decided we didn't have a prayer of succeeding, and financing became almost impossible."

Our woodworking entrepreneur has the last word. "Being black has made it hard on me to get into the places where the money is. I spend my own time and money getting there only to be turned down again. The other avenues open to the white brothers aren't open to me.

"I'm not good at speaking. I know I can't portray the knowledge I have in the business, and they look at you with one eye most of the time, like: 'What are you going to do with this money? You aren't going to do anything but throw it away . . . go to the track or something.' They don't realize I have ambitions, too. I want to explain that I will stay like I am. I haven't run off with money before. Why would I run off with theirs?"

IT'S A SMALL PIE

For the most part, our minority entrepreneurs were too caught up in their everyday problems to be able to look very far past the day's cash receipts. But one respondent, the bookstore owner, seemed to have thought about the place of minority capitalism in the overall economic scheme of things. And he concluded that small businesses were really not in the mainstream, that the minority community itself was chronically on the edge of poverty, that the future for any enterprise exclusively tied to that community was uncertain and marginal.

"Let me go downtown in Los Angeles, right in the middle of Bunker Hill, and do my thing," he challenged. "Then we can say the minority businessman is getting into the mainstream, that minority capitalism has begun. There's no money out here in the wasteland, brother, it's all down there in the center of the pie.

"We're living out here where white business rakes the money off and doesn't leave anything for the black community. The black man even goes to white areas to shop. How can there possibly be any money left in the ghetto for the black businessman?

"The place for minority capitalism if it's ever going to go anywhere, is down there with Mister Charlie."

5

LESSONS
FROM MOM AND POP—
REVEALING
CASE STUDIES

The possibility of some sort of program to support the development of small businesses of the "Mom-and-Pop" kind in East and South Central Los Angeles has generated a great deal of discussion and controversy. Clearly, however, past experience reveals such undertakings to be so marginal in their operations that they almost inevitably fail.

The six case studies in this section project much of the flavor of that precarious existence. But perhaps more important, they constitute a clear rebuttal to Professor Farmer's contention, set forth in Chapter 3, that business students can rescue the marginal small business by volunteering their freshly acquired acumen as consultants. Alas, the chronic undercapitalization and dearth of management skills that afflict these enterprises might well balk even an army of our best intentioned MBA candidates.

But there are other, more general, conclusions to be gained from the studies. Let us briefly examine these and then turn our attention to the cases themselves.

1. Even in the smallest businesses, there are many managerial functions whose counterparts are found in the largest businesses. Typically, those who start or operate small businesses are neither aware of all of these functions, nor do they perform most of them.

2. The business assistance needed by these small firms is not available except at prices they cannot afford.

3. The fundamental problems faced by these firms are typical of those faced by all small businesses. Racial problems constitute only a small part of the overall problem.

4. There is little possibility that these businesses will expand sufficiently to provide significant employment or necessary business services to local communities.

CASE I: F.E.D. & SONS*

Introduction

F.E.D. & Sons has been in business for more than nine years. It is an informal partnership of the owner, his wife, and their three adult sons. The chief function of the company is:
1. To service, clean, and repair ironing combs used primarily in the black hair-styling market.
2. To manufacture ironing combs.

Organization

The owner is a black man in his late forties to middle fifties. He entered the business as a partner in a heated comb manufacturing concern in an eastern city in 1949. Health problems brought him to California in 1959, at which time he began his own business. His gross revenue is now 60 percent from service and 40 percent from sales.

Staffing

The staff includes husband, wife, and the three adult sons who hold other full time jobs and work part time or as they are needed. The husband is manager and planner, while the wife concentrates on sales. Three days a week, she makes the rounds of the local beauty salons, seeking either to sell new combs or to sell the service of cleaning and adjusting combs already owned by the salons.

One of the boys, an accountant for a major corporation, does whatever accounting is needed. When he cannot, however, the owner "has an outside bookkeeper he runs to for needed work." All manufacturing or cleaning is done in a converted garage behind the home, with the husband doing the work. There are a "few" dealers in midwestern and eastern cities who handle out-of-state sales. There are, however, no exclusive arrangements, and orders are "received" only as these dealers themselves receive them. Dealers account for about 50 percent of manufacturing sales.

Direction

Because of the family nature of the organization, there is very little direction by the owners. Some thought has been given to the type of direction

---

*Names in all cases are fictitious, but the businesses are real.

needed should the firm expand enough to hire "outside" employees. At this stage, however, such thought has been confined to "the thinking process," with direction consisting of a simple division of labor.

Planning

To date, planning has been both informal and erratic. Advertising is through direct mail with no specific plan in mind. ("After you send out three or four mailers and get no response, you just give up for a while.") Most of the business comes from the weekly calls on the beauty salons in the city. Product planning is also very informal. It was the intention of the owner to design and manufacture a self-heating comb when he came to California in 1959. He still cherishes this ambition:

> I first started out when we came here by cleaning and repairing ironing combs with the intention of designing the first professional self-heating comb. From the business of cleaning and repairing, we started making simple ironing combs which must be heated on a stove. It looks now like we should be able to start selling the first self-heating combs by about the end of this year. What I want to do is get these self-heating combs on the market and build a national sales force so that we can stop making the "regular" combs. That will get us above the crowd and make us a lot better company.

The only other plans are to develop a heating curler that can be adjusted from one inch to three inches with about three sizes in between. There are no other plans or attempts to evaluate market conditions, although the owner feels that he will need financing to launch the new comb.

Control

The records of the company are adequate for controlling day-to-day financial requirements, but there appears to be little control over the planning of expenditures that might result in future profits. Due to the size of the company, employee control is no problem.

There is, however, a problem of control of five outside suppliers. Presently, there is a two-month delay on the delivery of raw materials, and some suppliers have been unable to meet quality standards despite repeated assurances. The smallness of the operation makes it almost impossible to force suppliers to comply.

Other Related Information

The new self-heating comb will probably have a retail price of around $60, and a manufacturing price of $24. (Present combs retail at about $5 with a manufacturing cost of about $2.)

The owner feels that there is great need to develop both an effective sales organization for this new comb and an advertising campaign that will get results. His capital is completely committed to meeting the daily costs of manufacturing and servicing "old style" combs. Capital is needed to develop the marketability of the new comb and to hire more workers. The new comb will have a 100-watt heating unit and will be backed by a 15-to-20 year guarantee. The owner anticipates recalling the combs every year for maintenance and check-up at a fee of $10. This charge will cover replacing all worn parts.

The firm has a $15,000 loan from the SBA, $12,000 of which is outstanding. All payments continue to be made on time. Approximate annual gross is estimated at $25,000. The market is estimated to have the following characteristics:

1. Over one million black beauticians in the United States.
2. About 600 beauty dealers who call on the U.S. black market.
3. Competition from only five suppliers world-wide: one in Germany, one in Japan and three in the United States. The German company is by far the largest.
4. Average retail price of each comb is about $5.
5. Distributor's discount is about 40 percent.
6. There are no professionally sold self-heating ironing combs.
7. Present national consumption of ironing combs is about one million, with no real knowledge of trends.

CASE II: ALFRED'S TAILORING

Introduction

Alfred's Tailoring is a sole proprietorship that has been in existence for more than three years. It is in downtown Los Angeles, very close to the campus of the University of Southern California. Services provided are mending and alterations. The owner is black, as are almost all of his clients.

Organization

Mr. Alfred, now in his middle to late thirties, has been a tailor for most of his working life. Until starting his own business at this location three years ago, he was a tailor at a large men's store. Business was very good the first year but has since showed a steady decline. Present gross is probably half the first year's level. This decline puts the proprietorship in a "just marginal" profit position. The shop is very small, about 40' x 40', with little room for such things as fitting and changing rooms. Mr. Alfred is changing the arrangement to give more area to fitting and changing and "improve the appearance."

Staffing

There are no other employees. Mr. Alfred has had employees at various times, but the business at the moment cannot justify anyone else.

Former employees confined themselves to simple mending. "It is very hard to find capable people who can do more than the very simple jobs," Mr. Alfred says. "I used to spend a great deal of my time just going over the mistakes of others." He is hopeful of getting someone so that he can spend more time on attracting new customers. Past employees have been hired through the California State Employment Service, but Mr. Alfred thinks he may advertise in the local newspaper next time.

Direction

Direction is looked upon as giving an employee a garment and telling him what must be done and the procedure to follow. The business as a whole does not have any formal direction, but rather grows or changes according to customer traffic through the shop.

Planning

Planning is on a very informal basis, although a great amount of thought is given to things that might help develop the business. However, it is very hard to implement this thinking. When the shop opened three years ago, a door-to-door handbill campaign was conducted in the neighborhood. The results were very encouraging, and more work came in than could be handled. Some thought has been given to conducting another such campaign, but as yet Mr. Alfred has been too busy to prepare for it.

Control

Control has been one of the biggest problems in the conduct of this business. From an accounting point of view, financial controls are exercised very infrequently. About every two or three months, an independent book-keeper comes in, picks up the sales slips and expense invoices, and prepares a record of cash flow and profit for that period. Profits or losses cannot be determined until this reckoning takes place.

Another control problem has resulted from customers' leaving garments for repair and never picking them up. Some garments have been left for over six months and attempts to locate the customer or sell the merchandise have failed. "The cost of mending a garment and not being paid for it is very high, and it is almost impossible to sell the items at any price," Mr. Alfred concedes. "Just yesterday I gave several large boxes of clothes to the Good Will because the items were unclaimed and could not be disposed of in any other way."

A third control problem is evaluating customer credit. Many of the early customers were those he had served at the department store. They had good jobs and paid their bills very well. Mr. Alfred says, "About a year after the business had been going I discovered that I had lost most of these customers and that most of the new customers were on relief. I would guess that about 80 percent of this neighborhood is on relief. I had no idea before I came here." Mr. Alfred also feels it is very hard to get new customers, although he has not made any systematic attempt to get new business.

Other Related Information

During the three years that Mr. Alfred has been in business, the cost of materials and rent has gone up from 20 to 30 percent. His prices have remained constant, although he expects to increase them in the near future. His major competitors are not other tailors, but rather dry cleaners who do cheaper work both on a price and quality basis. For example, a small mending job at Alfred's would cost $1.75 to $2, while the same job at the cleaners would be about $1.25. Mr. Alfred is looking for, and would appreciate, any ideas from business students to improve his profits. He would also like ideas on how he could expand by obtaining a loan. One suggestion has been to contact major department stores for their alteration requirements.

CASE III: ROD'S MARKET

Introduction

This small proprietary neighborhood grocery store has been in existence since March 1966. The nearest competitor is another "Mom-and-Pop" store, about twice the size of Rod's, one and one-half blocks away. There are two other small stores and a liquor store within a three-block radius. The nearest supermarket is about 10 blocks away. The average purchase at Rod's Market is between $1 and $2. Product lines consist of such frequently purchased items as milk, bread, meat, and wine.

Organization

The owner is a divorcee in her late twenties, who depends on the store for her livelihood. A cousin spends about 30 hours a week managing the store, and a teenage nephew works from 30 to 40 hours per week as clerk. Except for a butcher who was employed for a short time when the business first opened, these are the only people who have been part of the organization. All are blacks.

The proprietress was close to the food handling business as a girl when her family had a restaurant and wholesale food firm. She had no previous direct experience in food store marketing. The other two staff members are completely new to the business. The manager is responsible for ordering and estimating turnover. It is his intention to "show that the small store is just as good as the supermarket, and is, in fact, a better place to shop." Buying is through the Cash and Carry wholesale houses, because Rod's Market cannot get together the necessary cash to buy membership in a buying group. This means that their costs are somewhat higher than many "Mom-and-Pop" stores.

Staffing

Staffing has not been a problem because of the donated time of the manager and nephew. If business were to increase, there would be need for another person. Thought has been given to hiring someone whose job would be to go from door to door in the neighborhood and sell the benefits of shopping at Rod's. This would entail showing comparative prices, explaining services, and getting a feeling for the products and extent of line required. Nothing will be done until there is enough money to hire such a person.

Direction

Company direction is very informal and comes from the ideas of the manager and the expectations of the owner. There appears to be no goal or level of turnover toward which they are aiming.

Planning

Planning has been both informal and erratic. Several plans were laid out before the business began, but few of these have been implemented.

One plan that appeared to offer substantial profit was the installation of a fresh fish counter. None of the other stores in the area carry fresh fish, but there appears to be quite a demand, judging from the number of people who buy from a fish truck that comes through the neighborhood on occasion. Another plan was to install a chicken barbecue pit, but there was too little space. At this stage, both plans have been shelved. Other than the plan to send out a house-to-house sales person, no other advertising or promotion is planned or being carried out.

The SBA granted a $6,000 loan in 1967, an amount not really adequate to finance a complete improvement program. This loan was used mostly to increase stock (about $3,000) and to buy two freezers. Also needed was the ability to satisfy the capital requirements of one of the local buying associations so that purchases could be made more economically. However, Rod's was unable to meet either the $1,500 fee or to maintain a cash level of $1,000 in its banking account.

Control

Financial control is exercised through an outside accountant who does a bimonthly summary of transactions and estimates income taxes payable. There have been three different accountants since the business opened, each one replaced when it appeared that someone else could do the job better. One question the manager is now asking is: "What happens to the 20 percent gross we work towards; it just never shows up."

The manager feels that pilferage is a major problem, but he is unable to guess at the loss. Since the store is small, the person behind the counter can see everyone in the building. When things are very busy, however, it is quite easy for someone to slip out unnoticed with merchandise.

Other Related Information

The owner and the manager are both very interested in increasing their knowledge of the food store business but find it difficult to get to adult or extension classes. They would be very interested in having a university student develop a cost accounting system for the store and then explain how the system functions.

Rod's annual gross is about $52,000. This is very close to returns from the first year's operation, but is down some 30 percent from the second year.

Rod's has been approached a number of times by black militants who promised support if the business would have nothing whatsoever to do with either white suppliers or customers. The market has refused, and the manager feels that turnover has been negatively affected. Most of the customers in the area are on welfare (estimated at around 80 percent). It is felt that the present greatest need is for an increase in capital. The manager suggested that an additional $10,000 "would put the store in very good shape."

CASE IV: SOLID PLASTICS COMPANY

Introduction

Solid Plastics is an informal partnership between Mr. and Mrs. Roberts. Mr. Roberts has a BS in electrical engineering and worked in electronics while living in Chicago. Mrs. Roberts was with a plastics covering company.

On arrival in California about four years ago, the couple decided that the weak competition in the covering business made it a good opportunity. They started a business in their garage and moved to the present location about three years ago. There are about 10 competitors in the Southeast Central district, the closest about 20 blocks away. The product is used primarily by members of minority groups living in the ghetto area. The product line is simply described as plastic sheets sewed together to form coverings for cushions, couches, and chairs. Raw material comes from Japan with a 35-to-40-day delay. A couch cover takes about three hours to make.

Organization

The operation is housed in a 20' x 80' building, and machinery consists of four sewing machines and one plastic cutter. Mr. Roberts handles all the managerial responsibilities. Current net profit is about 22 percent. The owner estimates that a net profit as high as 30 percent could be realized if the business were operating at maximum efficiency.

Staffing

The staff consists of five cutters, one machine operator, a part-time secretary, and an outside accountant. Mr. Roberts is manager and salesman, and Mrs. Roberts oversees quality and production. Hiring is done through advertisements in the local paper or through contact with the State Department of Employment. Mr. Roberts states that although the work does not require a high degree of skill, it is still very hard to find competent employees.

The average employee has been there 30 months. Not many have quit. Over the last couple of years there have been times when business was very slow, and some of the employees were laid off. The lay-off process has some negative effects, one of which is difficulty in gearing up when business improves. The employees appear to work well together and as a group seem quite happy.

Mr. Roberts spends about half his time selling, largely through leads gained from advertising and from referrals from old customers. Referrals account for about 90 percent of new clients. Selling procedure is as follows: a prospective client is located; Mr. Roberts goes to the client's home and makes a rough cost estimate; on acceptance, he measures the item to be covered, roughly cuts out the plastic to be used, and makes the necessary fitting marks. The plastic is then taken back to the office where it is fine cut and sewn together. Mr. Roberts then delivers the finished item. The entire process takes from two to five days.

Direction

Direction, though informal, is more structured than the other cases studied. The training program consists of selecting a new employee and assigning him or her to an experienced operator for job training. Mr. Roberts then makes periodic checks to determine the level of performance. It is estimated that it takes about two to three months before the new employee becomes really productive. Mr. Roberts sets goals to increase his own performance and attends as many classes as possible through SBA or the University. He appears genuinely interested in improving his managerial performance.

Planning

Advertising is conducted on a fairly regular basis. So far, there has been no attempt to determine how effective the two-column, 4" ads are in producing customers. The owner has stated, however, that referrals appear to be satisfied with the product and price range and are therefore ready to do business. A harder sell is required to get commitment from clients gained from advertising.

Mr. Roberts feels that his business would prosper more if he could capture a few government contracts for such items as typewriter covers. To bid on these contracts, he needs some new heat sealing equipment. A team from the UCLA Graduate School of Business is working on a program to assist him in planning expansion.

During the first year or two of operation, Mr. Roberts carried most of his customers on contracts. However, the rapid expansion of the business required more capital, and he has since discounted most contracts to Dial Finance at a rate of about 10 percent. On several occasions the business has attempted to get loans or to bid on contracts but has been turned down on the grounds that its organizational structure is a deterrent. To be successful in these areas, the lenders said he should consider incorporation. Mr. Roberts is considering it.

Control

The business seems to be comparatively well-controlled. Accounting is done on a monthly basis by an outside CPA. Employees are closely watched for output and quality by both Mr. Roberts and his wife. At the present size of the business, "any problems can be identified before they become too big."

Other Related Information

Mr. Roberts considers financing for expansion as his greatest hurdle. He would like to find a salesman to take over some of his own selling time so that he could spend more time on planning. Mr. Roberts feels that it is harder for a black businessman to get loans than for a white one and that his customers are discriminated against when he tries to sell their contracts.

CASE V: QUALITY HOUSEHOLD PRODUCTS

Introduction

This company manufactures and sells a line of hand cleaners, furniture polish, floor wax, and a general purpose cleaner. It is in Lynwood Park and was incorporated in 1947.

Organization

Mr. B. James was a carpenter who lived next door to Quality. In April 1968, the original owner approached Mr. James and informed him that he was leaving the community and was *giving* the total business to Mr. James. After being informed of the gift of the business, Mr. James received one full day's instruction on running the operation. The previous owner then moved out of the community, and B. James became owner and manager.

Staffing

Until the time of the takeover by Mr. James, all selling was done by one traveling agent who sold for his own account. The staff had consisted of the previous owner, his wife, and two children. The present staff at Quality includes Mr. James, an office girl, a bookkeeper and as many as six teenagers from Willowbrook Job Corporation. The traveling agent continues to sell to accounts in the Northwest.

Mr. James wants to bring in a college student to learn the business and free him to spend more of his time on personal interests.

Direction

It has been very difficult for Mr. James to direct his new organization, for he is still unsure about how he wants it to run. A proposal by a consulting team from UCLA to stimulate local sales and thereby generate a fairly high cash flow was turned aside on the grounds that it would require him to make several sales calls per week. At this time, Mr. James is interested in setting up a franchise plan to sell the soap-making inputs and operating plans to minority organizations in other states and generate work for individuals who would otherwise be unemployed.

Planning

This organization is almost entirely without planning. Mr. James prefers to make moves and decisions on the spur of the moment and sees little benefit in advanced planning. While it is his intention to expand the business as much and as quickly as possible, he does not want to consider the ways that this could be accomplished. It is his feeling that the right direction for expansion will "just come along."

The Economic Development Center in Los Angeles was very impressed with the potential of Quality Products and was extremely interested in backing James with a loan if he would submit the normal financial statements. His reaction to this offer was, "Yes, he did need the money to expand, but the statements were too much work for him. They should be done by the Center."

Control

Financial control is almost completely lacking. While the profit margin is quite high on each item (about 17¢ cost of manufacture for a 5-lb. can of cleaner selling at $5 retail—wholesale price is 40 percent of retail), there is no control over the possibility of lowered selling prices and increased operating costs.

Other Related Information

Since taking over the business, Mr. James has yet to determine who his customers are or have been. For example, a few weeks after he acquired the business, a truck from Continental Airlines pulled up and the driver stated he was there for the monthly order of 50 cases. This was the first notice that Mr. James had had that Continental was a client—by luck there were 50 cases (no more) of general cleaning compound in stock.

A small study of past bills has revealed that the product has been sold all around the world and that a number of the large aerospace companies have been major purchasers. At this time, Mr. James does not intend to try and gain back these accounts or to determine why they stopped buying. Projected annual sales at current capacity are from $100,000 to $150,000. Expenses range from $40,000 to $50,000.

CASE VI: FRANK'S MEN'S AND BOYS' CLOTHING STORE

Frank's Clothing Store has been in operation on the main street of Watts for a number of years. However, prior to the Watts riots of 1965, it was owned and operated by a white man who apparently did very little to enhance his standing in the community.

After the riots, the store was reopened by Mr. Frank (a black) and has been under his operation for about two years. Mr. Frank has spent the greater part of his life in California, and attended the University of Southern California.

His college degree, however, was awarded by the University of Illinois. Most of Mr. Frank's 10 years of business experience was acquired at J.C. Penney Co.

The store has an area of about 40' x 120' and is one of only two clothing stores in the Watts community. On inspection of the store, and from discussions with Mr. Frank, it became apparent that he was in need of marketing assistance (both to develop and improve the layout, and more importantly, to find ways of tapping the majority of his potential customers who were shopping in other communities) and accounting assistance to improve his present recording procedures.

While Mr. Frank is faced with the normal problems of small business, inadequate inventory and scarce capital, he feels that his biggest problem is that of being a black man who must prove that the blacks can improve their positions without outside help from "Whitey." He stated that he appreciated having white students from UCLA offer business advice to him, but if he were to accept this assistance he would be reinforcing the old adage that "if it's going to be done right, it takes 'Whitey'." He did agree that he could very well use the assistance of the white students and that by turning their offer down he would be losing possible income.

Mr. Frank wants to improve his business. He wants to show the young blacks in the neighborhood that an education is important, and he wants to prove that the black man can operate without any help from whites. UCLA was unable to fulfill his request for a black student consultant because there was none available. It was Mr. Frank's feeling that by insisting on black assistance only he would be supported wholeheartedly by the black community and would thus not be a target in any future riot. Mr. Frank's store interior was completely demolished during the Watts Festival of 1968.

The single most inescapable reality dogging all efforts to create more minority business opportunities in South Central and East Los Angeles is the painful fact that the small businessman is almost an anachronism today. As yet this reality has been ignored by the agencies examined in this study. Too many of their programs do a disservice to minority aspirants by creating the impression that enthusiasm or ethnic solidarity are tolerable substitutes for business experience, education, or training.

In case after case we watched the minority businessman convert his ideas and drive into a small business under the assumption that he could negotiate financing from some private group or government agency. The cold fact is, he usually cannot—for any of a variety of reasons. We found little effort being made at this critical point to provide redirection or counseling on what the agency might view as a reasonable level of operations or expectations for minority businessmen. When the ethnic factor enters the picture, the risks seem to daunt even those agencies committed to high-risk ventures.

Coming to grips with lending criteria applied by the agencies appears to be another hurdle for the minority prospect. Although this study registered inputs from disparate and numerous private businessmen and government agency representatives, it was nonetheless impossible to determine with precision what criteria lenders and public agencies apply in selecting those businesses that are assisted. However, one of their bêtes noires is the traditional minority enterprise—i.e., anything retail-oriented or dealing in consumer service.

On the other hand, it appears that a firm is only considered eligible if it has a minimum number of employees (our experience indicates that this number ranges somewhere between 9 and 15 in most instances). But to compound the confusion, some of the businesses in the sample seemed to qualify in this and every other respect, yet never received financial assistance.

The conclusions of this study simply reinforce those of Dr. Brimmer. Most of the firms examined are clearly marginal—or submarginal—and may vanish overnight from the business scene. New firms that do enter the arena are making neither accurate nor reliable sales projections and tend to rely too much on limited markets. Any business founded on the assumption that it can serve a local market and be supported on a *profitable* level, simply because it is making a strong racial or social effort, is doomed to failure.

At this point it might be well to recall Dr. Brimmer's arguments, with the caveat that they are here modified to reflect lessons learned in Los Angeles:

1. The South Central and East Los Angeles economies do not offer a sufficient scale of business operations to permit the creation of new, profitable, and strong minority businesses.

2. The income levels of central city residents are at the lower end of the scale, and there is little likelihood that their economic status will improve enough to brighten investment potential for businesses in those areas.

3. The assumption that a black can create his own self-employment ignores the fact that he may have neither the education nor the experience nor the general understanding of business and economics to succeed.

4. The real future for blacks would seem to lie in learning something about business policies and programs by entering large businesses or corporations. In this way, they equip themselves to start a business of their own, with the assistance of some larger, more profitable business, or to enter an existing successful business with the intention of expanding or enlarging it.

5. The emphasis now being placed on minority capitalism, and the failures which seem to be related to it, are likely to discourage a great many minority entrepreneurs from attempting any kind of economic advancement or participation in the general economy.

6. Efforts to support minority capitalism in South Central and East Los Angeles are, to some extent, proving harmful to the community by encouraging high risks on the part of persons least equipped to take them. The high failure potential existing in these ventures places a burden on the local community, and disillusionment among those already in business or wishing to start is likely to make it increasingly difficult to introduce further worthwhile economic activity into South Central or East Los Angeles.

7. An appropriate goal in South Central Los Angeles probably should be to get all blacks into the mainstream of the general economy and *not* to encourage separate black activities that are likely to fail.

THE OUTLOOK IS FOR MERE SURVIVAL AT BEST

Having borrowed this framework from Dr. Brimmer, let us now apply our own findings to the question of survival and its alternatives. A constant fact of life among businessmen in South Central Los Angeles is that they may not be able to survive an additional day of business, usually because of their lack of working capital. Some kind of effort should be made to minimize the time between the application for a loan, say from the SBA, loan approval and disbursement of funds. A firm without working capital can hardly take much comfort in the knowledge that its application has been approved and that it will be receiving funds "in the future."

Even with this streamlining, however, the problem of inadequate capital will remain critical. Moreover, despite the passage of considerable time, the competitiveness of business markets has still not produced as diverse and high a level of commercial activity as that enjoyed by suburban communities. This compels the conclusion, then, that reviving the inner city is not so much a matter of taking advantage of unexploited opportunities as it is one of finding solutions to the grinding and relentless poverty that continues to scar South Central Los Angeles.

Efforts to strengthen black or Mexican-American or American Indian capitalism by the creation or enlargement of minority-dominated businesses serving minority communities seem doomed to failure at the present. Most of these efforts focus on small businesses where the failure rate is inordinately high, whatever the racial character of the community. The problem is exacerbated by the reality that minority groups have had so little opportunity for self-employment that it is quite uncommon for them either to think of accumulating the resources for such an activity, or to envision organizing or operating an activity for themselves. In the final analysis, we must set all this against our findings that the ghetto market potential simply does not exist. Any small business in South Central or East Los Angeles is a creature of narrow profit margins, high risks, and a monotonous effort merely to survive, much less expand.

THE AGENCIES—SOME CONCLUSIONS

What have we learned about the agencies active in advancing minority capitalism? The answer is "quite a lot," much of it at odds with official or popular versions of what has been taking place. The following conclusions represent the distillations of interviews with those who acquired their scars on the firing line.

1. All the programs have been given wide publicity, but there is a lack of hard evidence as to what they are really accomplishing. Frequently, the announced aims seem to be at variance with reported results. Moreover, the money invested in setting up and running some of the programs seems far too much for the results achieved.

2. Whatever the evidence may be on the effectiveness of the programs, there continues to be a very strong opinion among a large number of minority businessmen that they are beset with red tape that keeps them from getting the help they really need. There is even the feeling that perhaps these programs have been instituted and publicized more for political aggrandizement or personal benefit to the organization than for the purpose of developing minority businesses. On the other hand, there is good reason to believe that some of the misunderstanding about the purposes of these organizations and the things they can do arises from a failure of the ordinary minority businessman to understand what can and cannot be achieved within the resources and programs these organizations sponsor.

3. The agencies supporting the minority capitalism movement made it clear that they are not interested in providing support to the typical small-scale minority enterprise in the central city. For example, some of the firms will not provide capital or any support to any business that hires less than six persons or that is engaged in any kind of retailing or consumer service activity. This is unfortunate since many members of the minority community could, with minimal training, provide a variety of consumer services that are not now readily available to the community. This would include minor house repairs, gardening, house painting, and other kinds of repair or maintenance.

4. There are very few black enterprises operating in South Central Los Angeles that are able to employ 10 or more persons, possess management expertise, and are willing to accept assistance or even seek it from any of the agencies mentioned.

5. The small business assistance program has working capital requirements that simply cannot be met by most small minority businesses. The greatest benefits from the SBA, and its greatest successes, appear to be related to the 8A program that provides for subsidized bidding on government contracts. Perhaps equally successful are the M-1, M-2, M-3, M-4 and M-5 programs that train hard-core unemployed youths in their local area.

RECOMMENDATIONS FOR CHANGE

Perhaps the most important recommendation that could be made with respect to areas like South Central Los Angeles is that small businessmen should not be encouraged to undertake marginal business operations, particularly of the "Mom-and-Pop" service variety. Employment levels, family incomes, and general economic conditions in the area simply do not warrant this kind of answer to its economic problems.

A recommendation of only slightly less importance is that lenders who intend to operate in inner-city areas should appoint loan officers who will become intimately acquainted with the cultural, social, and economic facts of life in the inner city. The particular problems and processes of working with minority businesses must be recognized. These frequently run counter to general bank lending policies and, if imperfectly understood, can cause the best-intentioned bank lending programs to fail. Inner city loan officers should not only be fully aware of all the problems associated with financing the small business, but they should also be particularly well-acquainted with the special problems of minority-owned and -operated enterprises.

Our third recommendation arises from the finding that an insufficient amount of capital has been provided for inner-city programs. Too little additive effect has been obtained by those programs now in operation. Clearly, a great deal more could be achieved if all capital now flowing into the inner city could be pooled and its use coordinated. However, it must be remembered that provision of capital is only one small part of the total package needed to revive the economic potential of the inner city. Basically, those who want to start businesses need a full education in all aspects of organizing, operating, and producing a successful business.

Closely related to this is the recommendation that those who seek employment be educated in a variety of skills, from basic reading and writing to such subtle but important matters as attitude and willingness to accept certain constraints associated with operating in the normal business community.

Our fifth recommendation will seem as obvious as it has proved difficult of achievement. It is nevertheless an essential requirement. Minority businessmen do face discrimination in whatever they attempt to do. Sometimes this discrimination is direct and evident. At other times it is both subtle and covert. The experiences of some black businessmen interviewed clearly indicate that discrimination exists. It is essential, therefore, that those who work in the inner city acknowledge such discrimination and attempt to remedy it rather than ignore it.

The sixth recommendation is that any effort directed toward supporting minority capitalism should concentrate on encouraging businesses that can compete profitably in regional and national markets. More large companies should be encouraged to move into the inner city and set up small organizations modeled after their own operations. Ultimately, this should lead to establishing a subsidiary or creating a competitor whose focus will be on hiring minorities and developing a minority-owned and -operated corporation in markets where the appeal need not, and cannot, be solely to race.

Minority employment efforts appear to offer more potential for success, at less cost, than do minority capitalism efforts. The *experiences* that companies in South Central Los Angeles have had in *training* minorities for entry and for responsible management positions need to be documented fully, translated into educational and training programs, and introduced in the area through the schools. In the eyes of recipients, too, much of the public educational effort seems irrelevant, outdated, and unrelated to the actual employment problems that confront them in the real world.

Since federal efforts to date are neither well understood nor their results adequately communicated to prospective clients, more money should be invested in federal programs and more effort should be made by the federal government to use the expertise and good offices of local private businessmen. The inputs of minority businessmen in the area should be encouraged so that the result provides a more efficient use of available funds and agencies.

When government assistance programs are announced, the criteria for receiving assistance should be made very explicit. Goals and requirements of the programs should be publicized widely and applied consistently. The operations of every agency in South Central Los Angeles should be open to constant inspection, and every effort should be made by these agencies to contact the local community and make known their policies, their programs, and other assistance available.

WHITHER WE GO

By any index South Central Los Angeles and East Los Angeles rate very poorly in terms of income, family composition, education, employment, housing conditions, and employment potential. The incomes of blacks, for example, are consistently lower than those for white families, whatever the basis of comparison used. The number of black families in South Central Los Angeles has more than tripled in the past 16 years, and there is every indication that this trend will continue. Most blacks who live in the western United States are living in California, will continue to live there, and are likely to remain concentrated, along with newcomers, in the cores of major cities, particularly Los Angeles, San Francisco, and Oakland.

There is a serious question as to whether present efforts are great enough to make even small inroads on the solution of inner-city problems. Some would argue that mastering job skills and getting a job are far more important to an inner-city resident than where the job is located, whether he has capital to start a new business, or whether his home is first-quality. Far too often, the evidence suggests that programs to foster minority capitalism have ignored, or been oblivious to, the economics of job creation, minority employability, and the basic educational reforms these goals require.

A

EXPERIENCE
OF LOS ANGELES
EMPLOYERS
WITH MINORITY
GROUP EMPLOYEES*

This study was conducted by the University of Southern California Research Institute for Business and Economics, the research arm of the USC Graduate School of Business Administration. The purpose of the study was to follow up the experience of (a) business firms which hired blacks from South Central Los Angeles after the riots of August 1965, and (b) the subsequent experience of the blacks hired at that time.

The results are encouraging. Personnel directors and first-line supervisors agree that black employees are much like other employees with respect to most measures of job performance. Turnover has been about the same as—or better than—among other employees. All of the personnel directors say that their experience has caused them to plan to hire at least as many minority group employees as in the past, and one-third plan to hire more. Expected problems with supervision and fellow workers have failed to materialize.

Employment standards are still a problem. Many firms require a high school education or the passing of written tests. The evidence indicates, however, that employers are increasingly recognizing the special cultural problems of the black community. Police records, for instance, are beginning to be scrutinized on an individual basis and the nature of the job being applied for taken into account.

The blacks who were placed have done relatively well. Two-thirds are still on the job, and almost all of these said the job was better than others they had had in the past. Half of the one-third who have left the jobs in which they were originally placed have found better jobs. Most have received pay increases or promotions. None of those who had left their original jobs gave discrimination as the reason.

About one-third of the blacks interviewed had moved their place of

*William H. Reynolds. "Experience of Los Angeles Employers with Minority Group Employees," Graduate School of Business Administration Report to Management No. 16, University of Southern California, March 1967

residence since being employed; almost all who had moved said their new home was better.

Lack of education and training, according to both employers and black employees, is the principal factor holding back black employment. One impression gained from the study is that it is basic education and pre-vocational training that constitute the principal lacks, and that employers stand ready to provide training in specific skills to trainable employees.

Most employers think blacks are as promotable as other employees, but some still seem to think of blacks as less promotable than other employees. This may reflect a combination of the actual lower level of education among many black employees and a residuum of stereotyped thinking.

Positive recruitment efforts are required to reach prospective black employees, and the study suggests that few firms try to provide any special counseling, help with transportation, or in any other way treat their black employees differently from the way they treat their other employees. Present efforts by employers in recognizing and acting upon the problems arising from the cultural environment of the disadvantaged black should continue and be expanded.

Major Conclusions

The Employees

1. The black employees interviewed were a relatively good sample of the black population of South Central Los Angeles. The data obtained on age, education, length of residence in Los Angeles, etc., are reasonably consistent with internal California State Employment Service analyses. It should be emphasized, however, that the sample was not representative in at least two ways. First, all of the respondents were at least sufficiently motivated to find work to register with the State Employment Service (although some registered only after employers began active recruiting). Second, the respondents were immediately employable, or at least were considered so by the firms that hired them. Nevertheless, all of those interviewed were people who were looking for jobs and were helped to find them.

2. Once on the job, the black employees seem to have done well. Two-thirds were still with the firms that had originally hired them, and, among these employees, about half had been promoted and almost all had received pay increases. (In many cases, no doubt, the pay increases were due to company policies providing for automatic increases after so many months on the job.) Their median wage was $2.75 an hour and almost all said that their present job was better than other jobs they had had in the past.

3. One-third of the blacks placed were no longer with the firm that had originally hired them. (This was 6 to 14 months after they were hired.) About half of those who had left their jobs were working elsewhere and in many instances described their present job as better. About 15 percent were unemployed again at the time of interview. In effect, positive results were obtained in the case of approximately 80-85 percent of the blacks placed.

4. Not one of the employees who had left the jobs in which they had been placed said that they left because of discrimination. (Recall that they were being interviewed by other blacks.) Their replies were frank. One respondent said: "There was no future with the company. It wasn't discrimination though. There wasn't any future for anybody." Another said simply that he was caught sleeping on the job. Perhaps the most significant difference between the employees who had stayed with the companies that had hired them and the employees who had left (either voluntarily or not) was that the former group were placed in higher paying jobs. Most of the employees who had left had been in jobs paying less than $2.00 an hour.

5. The blacks in the sample did not seem especially concerned about job discrimination. Only about 10 percent mentioned discrimination when asked if the company hiring them had given them an opportunity based on their ability and performance. Similarly, when asked specifically what they saw as the major factor holding back black employment, only 20 percent said discrimination. Almost monotonously, the respondents said lack of education, lack of training, lack of experience, lack of skill, lack of qualifications.

This is important. It points up the fact that the black community itself—or a major segment of it—believes that education and training is an answer to black unemployment and under-employment.

The Personnel Directors and First Line Supervisors

1. No less than 26 different organizations, agencies, and groups were named by the personnel directors when they were asked what private or public agencies they had worked with in hiring minority group employees.

2. All the firms interviewed have listed job openings with the California State Employment Service Centers, most have worked with other organizations trying to place minority group employees, most have advertised in minority group newspapers, most have sent recruiters into minority group neighborhoods, and almost all have tried to use their present minority group employees to recruit other minority group employees.

3. On the other hand, the study produced some evidence which would indicate a continuing need for employers to evaluate employment standards and tests as they relate specifically to actual jobs. For example, is a high school certificate required for certain jobs? Do the tests that are administered tend to bar some minority group applicants from being given the opportunity to get into a job? In fact, do the standards and tests tend to limit the supply of manpower that would prove to be productive if more realistic measures were used? Few tests are culture-free, and personnel directors tend to agree that blacks and Mexican-Americans do not do so well on the tests used as other applicants. Some companies, including several of the largest in California, are developing standards which relate more specifically and realistically to the requirements of the job.

4. Most firms said they try to treat minority group employees exactly like other employees. More recognition should be given to the problems arising from the cultural environment of the black community.

5. With respect to performance on the job, personnel directors and first line supervisors agreed the blacks and Mexican-Americans were much like other

employees. First line supervisor ratings of minority group members were somewhat higher than personnel director ratings on a list of job performance factors.

Only about one out of five personnel directors and only about one out of ten members of first line supervision felt that blacks required more training than other employees.

6. Turnover among blacks and Mexican-Americans was reported to be about the same as among other employees. The number of minority group employees who received pay increases or promotions was also reported as about the same as in the case of other employees. Overwhelmingly, poor education and the lack of basic qualifications were cited as the principal factors holding back minority group employment. About 10 percent of the personnel directors and first line supervisors also mentioned "poor attitude" as a problem among blacks and about 15 percent mentioned "language" as a problem among Mexican-Americans.

7. Generally speaking, the experience of companies that have hired blacks and Mexican-Americans has been significantly favorable. About one-third said that their experience has caused them to plan to hire more minority group employees in the future than they had in the past and about two-thirds said they planned to hire about the same number as in the past. None said they planned to hire fewer.

B

THE URBAN LEAGUE
TRAINING CENTER

Conceived by the Los Angeles Urban League and supported by the Bank of America and IBM, this program to train the disadvantaged in data processing skills made its debut in September 1968. The Center, usually called "ULTC," offers courses in keypunch, business programming, and operating computers and peripheral equipment. A comprehensive clerical skills program was under consideration in July 1971, the time of the interview on which this appendix is based.

The bank provides rent-free classroom, laboratory, and administrative space in a 22,000-square-foot building at 7226 South Figueroa Street in South Central Los Angeles. IBM has equipped the facility with such third generation hardware as an S/360 Model 30 computer, tape drives, printers, keypunch machines, and terminals. Overall, the estimated value of the complex is $1 million.

IBM has also detached one of its young executives, Karl G. Jefferson, to manage the program. An Air Force veteran, Jefferson holds a BS degree in physics and an MBA, both from UCLA. He is a native of Los Angeles and a product of local elementary and secondary schools. His staff includes three experienced data processing professionals, an administrative secretary, and a placement director.

"The Center considers placement every bit as important as training," Jefferson says. "We're not really helping unless our graduates are working. And until they are, our job isn't done."

Placement efforts have been seriously complicated by the downturn in aerospace and defense activity in Southern California. Ironically, this cutback struck at roughly the same time ULTC was launching its first classes. It has since continued, creating a situation that often finds Center graduates competing for jobs with more experienced workers recently laid off by firms in the area. Nevertheless, ULTC's placement record is striking. Records show, however, that some relocations have been necessary. Center graduates have moved to Northern California, the Midwest, Northeast, and the Washington, D.C., metropolitan area.

TABLE 3

ULTC Placement Record

Skill	No. Graduates	No. Placements	Percent
Business programmers	75	65	87
Computer operators	109	105	96
Keypunch operators	158	150	95
All categories	342	320	94

Source: Official ULTC records.

Instructional emphasis is intensely practical, reflecting as faithfully as possible both conditions and problems graduates will face on jobs in business. The keypunch class lasts five weeks and covers 029 card punch and 059 verifier. There is exposure to alphanumeric keys and alternate program drum coding, and the students spend their final two weeks working with "live" data in a realistic office environment. At graduation, their average speed is between 8,000 and 10,000 key strokes per hour.

The business programming curriculum includes flowcharting, coding, data base development, program testing and debugging, and program document-ation. Work is in basic COBOL, leading to mastery of American National Standard (ANS) COBOL, a leading compiler used in business programming. Students become familiar with the SORT and REPORT GENERATOR features of ANS COBOL and with both the small and minicomputer installations now gaining favor in business.

Computer operators spend six weeks in "hand-on" training in the ULTC computer center. This exposure provides familiarization with a typical S/360 machine room configuration, from the computer itself right on down to the keypunches that represent the starting point of the data processing cycle. ULTC computer operators know Input/Output (I/O) operations, job control, and basic programming concepts.

Jefferson feels that the ULTC approach has been generally well-received in the community and that its graduates are regarded as both qualified and highly motivated. *Southern California Business* called the ULTC program "one of the most successful and one of the most professional training programs of its kind in the nation." More than 130 firms have hired Center graduates.

BOOKS

Bell, Carolyn Shaw. *The Economics of the Ghetto*. New York: Pegasus, 1970.

Cross, Theodore L. *Black Capitalism: Strategy for Business in the Ghetto*. New York: Atheneum, 1969.

National Industrial Conference Board, Inc. *National Conference on Corporate Urban Programs: An Investment in Economic Progress and Social Order*. Proceedings of Conference, The Waldorf-Astoria, January 10, 1968. New York: the Board, 1968.

Wilson, James Q. *Negro Politics: The Search for Leadership*. New York: The Free Press, 1960.

ARTICLES

Shain, Richard A. "Two Approaches to Entrepreneurship: Keith Williams, The Hollingsworth Group," *MBA*, IV, (April 1970), 38-42.

Winters, William R., Thomas A. Klein, and Allen G. Brunner. "Minority Enterprise and Marketing: An Annotated Bibliography," *Council of Planning Librarians*, Exchange Bibliography No. 185, (April 1971), 1-39.

GOVERNMENT PUBLICATIONS

California Department of Industrial Relations, Division of Fair Employment Practices. *Negro Californians*. San Francisco: the Department, 1963.

California Department of Industrial Relations, Division of Fair Employment Practices. *Negroes and Mexican Americans in South and East Los Angeles*. San Francisco: the Department, 1966.

County of Los Angeles Commission of Human Relations. *The Urban Reality: A Comparative Study of the Socio-economic Situation of Mexican-Americans, Negroes, and Anglo-Caucasians in Los Angeles County.* Los Angeles: the Commission, 1965.

Housing and Home Finance Agency. *Potential Housing Demands of Non-White Population in Selected Metropolitan Areas.* Washington, D.C.: the Agency, 1962.

U.S. Bureau of the Census. *Current Population Reports,* Series P-23, No. 24, BLS Report No. 332, "Social and Economic Conditions of Negroes in the United States," (Washington, D.C., 1967).

_____ *Current Population Reports,* Series P-23, No. 26, BLS Report No. 347, "Recent Trends in Social and Economic Conditions of Negroes in the United States." Washington, D.C.: the Bureau, 1968.

_____ *Current Population Reports,* Series P-23, No. 29, BLS Report No. 375, "The Social and Economic Status of Negroes in the United States." Washington, D.C.: the Bureau, 1969.

_____ *Current Population Reports*, Series P-20, No. 210, "Mobility of the Population of the United States: March 1969 to March 1970." Washington, D.C.: the Bureau, 1971.

_____ *Current Population Reports*, Series P-20, No. 218, "Household and Family Characteristics: March 1970." Washington, D.C.: the Bureau, 1971.

_____ *Current Population Reports,* Series P-23, No. 18, "Characteristics of the South and East Los Angeles Areas: November 1965." Washington, D.C.: the Bureau, 1966.

_____ *Current Population Reports,* Series P-23, No. 27, "Trends in Social and Economic Conditions in Metropolitan Areas." Washington, D.C.: the Bureau, 1969.

_____ *Current Population Reports,* Series P-23, No. 33, "Trends in Social and Economic Conditions in Metropolitan and Nonmetropolitan Areas." Washington, D.C.: the Bureau, 1970.

_____ *Current Population Reports*, Series P-60, No. 58, "Year-Round Workers with Low Earnings in 1966." Washington, D.C.: the Bureau, 1969.

_____ *Minority-Owned Businesses: 1969,* MB-1. Washington, D.C.: the Bureau, 1971.

U.S. Bureau of Labor Statistics. *Changes in Urban America,* BLS Report No. 353. Washington, D.C.: the Bureau, 1969.

_____ *Poverty Areas of Our Major Cities,* Special Labor Force Report No. 75. Washington, D.C.: the Bureau, 1966.

_____ *Urban Employment Survey,* Report No. 2, Chicago, "Poverty—The Broad Outline." Washington, D.C.: the Bureau, 1970.

_____ *Urban Employment Studies,* Regional Report No. 18, "Employment and Unemployment in East and South Central Los Angeles." Washington, D.C.: the Bureau, 1971.

_____ *Work Experience of the Population in 1968,* Special Labor Force Report 115. Washington, D.C.: the Bureau, 1970.

U.S. Department of Commerce, Office of Minority Business Enterprise. *Directory of Private Programs Assisting Minority Business.* Washington, D.C.: the Department, 1970.

ABOUT THE AUTHOR

FREDERICK E. CASE, since 1961 professor of housing, real estate, and urban land economics at the Graduate School of Management, University of California, Los Angeles, obtained his master's degree and his doctorate in business administration from Indiana University. A member and former director of UCLA's Housing, Real Estate, and Urban Land Studies Program, Dr. Case has served also as president of the American Real Estate and Urban Economics Association, president of the Western Regional Science Association, and chairman of the committee to develop a two-year integrated MBA program at the UCLA Graduate School of Management. Dr. Case has presented papers, lectured, and conducted seminars before academic, governmental, and professional groups throughout the United States, Europe, and the Far East; in 1957-58 he was visiting professor at the Post-Graduate Institute of Business Administration, Turin, Italy, and at Rathmines College and the Irish Management Institute in Dublin. He has been guest lecturer for the American Institute of Real Estate Appraisers and the Society of Residential Appraisers on various campuses on the subject of real property evaluation theory. In addition to his several books, Dr. Case is the author of numerous research monographs, articles, and book reviews dealing with real estate, urban land economics, and related subjects, and is the former editor of *California Management Review*. In 1968, Dr. Case was the recipient of a grant from the Ford Foundation, International and Comparative Studies, to study European programs for housing the underhoused in Europe and Japan. He is the editor of *Inner-City Housing and Private Enterprise,* published by Praeger in Spring, 1970.